ESCAPE FROM
ARNHEM

ESCAPE FROM ARNHEM

A Glider Pilot's Story

GODFREY FREEMAN

Pen & Sword
AVIATION

First published in Great Britain in 2010 by
Pen & Sword Aviation
An imprint of
Pen & Sword Books Ltd
47 Church Street
Barnsley
South Yorkshire
S70 2AS

ISBN 978 1 84884 147 5

A CIP catalogue record for this book is
available from the British Library

Printed and bound in England
By CPI Antony Rowe, Chippenham, Wiltshire

Pen & Sword Books Ltd incorporates the Imprints of Pen & Sword
Aviation, Pen & Sword Family History, Pen & Sword Maritime, Pen &
Sword Military, Wharncliffe Local History, Pen & Sword Select, Pen &
Sword Military Classics, Leo Cooper, Remember When, Seaforth
Publishing and Frontline Publishing

For a complete list of Pen & Sword titles please contact
PEN & SWORD BOOKS LIMITED
47 Church Street, Barnsley, South Yorkshire, S70 2AS, England
E-mail: enquiries@pen-and-sword.co.uk
Website: www.pen-and-sword.co.uk

'Men fear death as children fear to go in the dark and as that natural fear in children is increased with tales, so is the other.'

Francis Bacon (1561–1626) Essays, 2. 'Of Death'.

Acknowledgements

This book is dedicated, not least, to all those friends and brave personnel of the Airborne Regiment, past and present, with their special qualities and spirit as well as those who fought and continue to operate equally bravely above, beneath and alongside them.

To name a very special few of them:

Lieutenant Henry Cole
Willem and Hennie Zieglers and family
The Dutch Resistance in its entirety
Major Coke
Pat Mahoney
Major Ian Toler

My thanks extend also, but not limited, to the following for their unfailing support in later days:

Henk Duinhoven and Marion Meffert
My sister Mary Sansbury MBE
My former family, Sheila, Mark and Karl Freeman
Bob Somerscales, GPR – Operation Overlord, Normandy
Arthur Proctor GPR and former chief flying instructor of the Upward Bound Trust, Haddenham Airfield, Thame, Oxon

The Upward Bound Trust [ubt.org.uk] is a voluntary organisation founded by ex-members of the Glider Pilot Regiment in the early 1960s, who continue to introduce young people to the air, in gliders, at a minimal cost.

My final and equally important thanks go to YOU for taking an interest and reading this book.

Contents

Introduction

A growing number of people have at last prevailed upon me to write this history. I have hesitated now for more than thirty-six years for a variety of reasons. Chief among them are two. One is that so many accounts of this kind have come before the public in the post-war years and the second is that I have feared to produce what amounts in current parlance to be no more than an 'ego trip', a tale of 'the great I am', a swaggering narrative depicting the author on a hero's progress through heroic events.

I make no claim to heroism, nor will my nature ever amount to that of a hero. I wish only to present myself as what I was, a human being in a human situation; a very young and immature human being faced with and perplexed by fears, idealistic conceptions of courage, dread of shame at being judged as less than one's peers, and an obsessive adolescent yearning to prove oneself a 'Man'.

Where then must this story begin? On reflection, the best place to begin seems to be the cellar of the municipal waterworks office building, opposite the northern end of the Colonel Frost Bridge at Arnhem, on the night of 20 September 1944.

CHAPTER 1

The Last Days at Arnhem Bridge

It is dark now. The heavy guns have stopped. The relays of tanks that have been bombarding our building from near point-blank range have ceased fire. Our building is on fire for the fifth time, or is it the sixth? We no longer have any means to put the fire out. There is no water. In our cellars we have over a 120 wounded, twenty-two of them German and a dozen or so Dutch civilians who have taken shelter with us. There is an all-pervading stench of blood, faeces and urine, the only approximation to a latrine being an oil drum full to the brim with stale urine with faeces floating on top. I cannot speak for the state of mind of those about me. I only know that I am in a dream world of exhaustion and have had no adequate sleep for four days and three nights. Last night a paratroop Sergeant Major gave me a 'Wakey-Wakey' pill so that I could take charge of the German prisoners. I am now bewildered and confused but fully aware that the situation is dire. Upstairs, small-arms ammunition is exploding like jumping squibs on Guy Fawkes Night. Next to the Dutch civilians, standing upright like outsize altar candles, are a few rounds of six-pounder anti-tank ammunition abandoned for want of a gun to fire them from. The implication of the fire hazard seems obvious to all but the Dutch, or is their brand of stoicism more deeply ingrained than ours? A paratrooper died in that room yesterday, or was it the day before? He died very quietly, with dignity, almost humbly. Hit in the stomach, he had sat there holding his wound and I had lit a cigarette for him. A little while later, I went back to see how he was getting on. His cigarette had gone out, but as I stooped to relight it for him, he made no movement. Both he and the cigarette, it seemed, had burnt out together.

My last glimpse of Colonel Frost occurred at about this time. White as wax from loss of blood, he lay on a kind of stretcher, defiant and coherent to the last. The bitterness in his voice was unmistakeable as he ordered the white sheet of surrender to be hoisted over the front of the building. Years later I was to be reminded of him when a thoughtless Persian hunter shot a hawk out of the sky. The hunter strode over to finish off the hawk with the butt of his shotgun, and the hawk, with its last dying strength, tore indelible talon scars on the elegant woodwork of the stock. Frost's defiance and the hawk's were identical in their intensity. No less indelible were the scars left by Frost's force on the enemy.

Down the cellar steps now comes the first of the *Waffen* SS. With his sub-machine gun at the ready, he inquires 'Are you British or American?' There is hidden significance in this question, for the American Airborne forces to the south had sworn to avenge the massacre of their comrades at St Mère-Église and were reputed to have taken no prisoners. 'We're British,' I replied. 'So what?' echoed a voice behind me. The SS man shouldered his gun and slapped me on the back as though I were a member of a visiting football team. 'Tommy!' he cried, with a huge grin of combined relief and apparent affection, 'Tommy! Tommy!'

But this was no time to fraternise. The fire was already devouring the building. What happened next might seem to illustrate the futility of war. With no perceptible hesitation and as though they had been training together throughout their service lives, British and German troops combined in a joint rescue operation to clear every living person from the cellars. Doors were ripped off nearby buildings to provide makeshift stretchers. Often mixed pairs of Airborne and SS men struggled together to lug the wounded out from certain death. A Hohenstaufen soldier and I checked the blazing upper floors as far as we could penetrate, and then clattered down to the cellar to find it empty and deserted. As we scampered out through the main entrance, a huge crackling beam crashed to the floor in a shower of sparks not ten paces behind us. Involuntarily, we both spun round to glance back. There was no need for words. We both raced across the road to the grass embankment opposite.

The wounded were laid temporarily side by side on the grassy bank where, here and there, the corpses of German soldiers who had ventured to break cover now lay uncollected. By now the flames were roaring, turning the abandoned building into a furnace. A tiny piece of debris whined over the road and landed harmlessly on my boot. The soldier on the stretcher at my feet lay face upwards, his eyes heavily bandaged. I had no further use now for my steel helmet so I took it off and covered his face.

In small groups the wounded were carried up the embankment, across the road, and down another bank on the far side. We wended our way among more German corpses, steered by that strange instinct that forbids stepping on the dead. One of them must have been lying there for more than a day or two. I recall that his stomach was so bloated that it had burst nearly all the buttons off his tunic, and to this day the image is still vivid in my mind's eye. A British Medical Officer was directing operations with a vehemence and authority that struck even the SS with awe. The medics' valour in that operation must surely by now have become a legend in the RAMC.

Down on the far side of the embankment, one of the first British I recognised was my flight commander, Captain Simpson. Almost at the same moment I caught sight of an SS officer standing close beside us, staring at the top of the embankment, and it was as though a camera shutter clicked inside my head. Silhouetted sharply in pitch black against the orange red fire glow in the sky was the now historic profile of the German soldier of World War Two; the characteristic helmet with the jutting peak and neck brim, the chin thrust out and up in implacable hostility, a stick grenade swinging in his right hand. Were I an artist I could paint that profile today, so starkly did it imprint itself on my brain; the archetypical, the very soul and essence of the ancient *Furore Teutonicus*.

'*Was ist los?*' asked Simpson. 'What's the matter?'

'*Ist nichts los*,' snapped the SS man impatiently. 'Nothing.'

In the near distance sporadic small-arms fire could still be heard. God knows who was holding out now or where. I asked if anyone had seen anything of Henry Cole, my skipper.

'I was going to ask you the same,' replied Simpson.

'And Major Jones – the anti-tank Major we brought over?' I asked. Simpson indicated a figure lying on his back close by.

'Over there,' he said. Rocking from side to side like a contented infant and humming what sounded like snatches of song was the barely recognisable person of the Battery Commander.

'What…?' I began.

'Bomb happy,' replied Simpson tersely.

Even in the darkness the Major's face was clearly lined and puffy with appalling fatigue.

'Hello Major,' I said. To my astonishment he recognised me instantly.

'Hello,' he replied, 'where's the old Yellow Scarf?' It was his nickname for Henry Cole, who liked to wear a yellow scarf decorated with foxes' heads.

'I'm afraid I don't know,' I said, 'I haven't seen him for two days. We got separated.'

Just then some louder explosions boomed out from nearby. Major Jones began to chortle and chuckle with bizarre inner content.

'There's a good one!' he almost cheered, as a much louder explosion sounded close by. His body shuddered with each explosion but he bore no sign of a wound. I took comfort from that and the fact that whatever had happened to him had left him remarkably cheerful.

Meanwhile, Captain Simpson appeared to have developed a severe limp. I looked down and saw a large dressing bound around his ankle.

'I didn't realise you had been hit,' I said apologetically.

'Don't be a bloody fool,' he whispered as loudly as he dared, 'I haven't been. This is a fake!'

'A fake?'

'To get into hospital of course!'

The spectacle of my Flight Commander brazenly swinging the lead was too much for my enfeebled mind to grasp.

'What on earth for?' I asked.

'Because my dear Freeman,' he explained, in the sort of tone commonly reserved for backward children or the very naïve, 'it is easier to get out of a hospital than it is to get out of a prison camp.'

My mind suddenly found a kind of second wind.

'That's a bloody good idea,' I said admiringly. 'I've still got a field dressing left. I can put it on my wrist.'

'Oh no you don't,' retorted Simpson 'I thought of it first!'

The reply was uttered in quite playful tones but it had its point. With two of us playing the same game our chances of getting away with it would be halved to say the least. Wild schemes began to flicker through my mind like the jerky frames of an old-fashioned film projector. In the midst of one of these fantasies I found myself looking down again at Major Jones and took a snap decision.

'All right,' I said, 'From now on I'm bomb happy, so please take no notice of anything I say or do from this moment on.'

'OK,' agreed Simpson, 'I'll back you up all I can.'

So began nearly four weeks of the most demanding role that I have ever played on amateur stage or indeed anywhere else. Thank God that I had Major Jones to learn from. Without his unwitting help as a living model, I know that my unrehearsed performance could never have survived more than a few days at the most. If he or any of his relatives ever read this account, I wish them to know of the debt of gratitude that I still acknowledge. I am happy to say that I learnt quite a long time afterwards that he made a complete recovery.

During the next few hours while we were being carted about together, barring short gaps when overcome with sleep, I don't think that I took my eyes off him for any longer than a minute at any one time. Then we became separated. Officers of field rank, when taken prisoner, were quickly removed from the presence of other ranks whom it was feared they might spur to turn on their captors.

The behaviour of a severely shell-shocked or 'bomb happy' man is often not unlike that of a drunk, morose or merry. He blunders against obstacles, staggers now and again, rambles incoherently or disjointedly and reacts to sudden noises with tremors, either coarse or fine in proportion to the volume of sound. Above all, his eyes have a staring, perplexed and uncomprehending look about them, like the eyes of a man stunned or half blind with drink. Very often, too, his mouth droops open, giving him an air of idiocy. Anyone with the slightest histrionic ability can ape these symptoms, but to overplay them or 'ham' them I knew would give the game away. They had to be spaced out with periods, long or short, but never consistent, of apparent calm and lucidity and occasional bouts of tearfulness. This was my part. The script had to be made up as the play went on.

Quite soon a group of us were moved in transport to a field dressing station whose name I have never discovered. The interior, with blacked out windows, was illuminated cautiously with candles and an odd oil lamp or two. Major Jones was laid on some sort of couch and I sat in a hard wooden chair behind it. Not more than six feet away from us a small table had been formally laid for the German Medical Officer in charge who shortly took his place and dined alone, apparently unconcerned and in the manner of one to whom formal dinners are daily routine. It would be easy to condemn that man as callous, but how long had he been on duty? Forty-eight hours? Seventy-two? The boiler has to be stoked if the engine is to run. He needed that dinner if he were to cope with what had now become a constant stream of new arrivals, and to survive, he needed to remain detached. Picking up his glass of wine, he held it like a test tube to a candle to examine its contents, drained it and stood up. A glance at Major Jones and myself assured him that neither of us were urgently in need of attention, a nurse spoke quietly to him and shook her head and he moved off silently into the shadows and the darkness where now and again groans and cries of pain could be heard.

I think at this moment I must have fallen asleep, but time had for some while ceased to bear any significance on events and all I knew next was that it was daylight. Slumped and stiff on the wooden armchair, I straightened to sit up, and then the recollection came crashing back like a thunderclap. I must not move or act normally. I must not look alert. Major Jones was no longer on the sofa. I went into a slump again and waited for the next cue.

After a while, a young Dutch nurse came and shook me gently by the arm and I went into the incoherent mumbling act. This was terrible and I was seized with frightful pangs of guilt. I had counted on deceiving enemy doctors, enemy medical orderlies, and enemy hospital staff. To play games with the staunchly loyal and sincerely sympathetic Dutch was a necessity I had not had the wit to foresee and was now abhorrent. As she led me down a corridor lined on either side by our own wounded, guilt was reinforced. Every moment spent with her meant time wasted on their behalf. For some moments I was tempted to throw in my hand, tell her I was a fake and have done with the whole charade, but one thought alone sustained me. I had come to know well in the past few days the calibre of the men who lay on those stretchers and knew that had they known what I was up to, every one would have urged me to keep up the effort. Given the unhampered use of his limbs, every man there would have made an escape bid one way or another. 'Don't be so bloody soft,' they would have told me. 'Don't mind us, you get the hell out of it while you can.' Chastened by humility, I continued down the corridor. The nurse guided me to the porch and I sat down on a bench in the blessed September sunshine.

Not many miles away heavy guns were still booming but there was now no sound of small-arms fire. A light early morning mist was veiling the trees, each one like an autumn bride, but there was an absence of birdsong. Not knowing who might be watching, I played safe with a few minor convulsions in time to the gunfire. Soon the nurse reappeared with a mug of acorn coffee and a half slice of komisbrot, the German Army bread that looked like it was peppered with woodlice. I tried to remember when I had last eaten or drunk anything. The jeep on which we had ridden into Arnhem on Sunday had disappeared by morning, together with our Bergen rucksacks containing, amongst other things, our ration packs and water bottles. On the Monday afternoon, or maybe the Tuesday, I had eaten some cheese and sardines from a captured German truck. There had been some bottles of wine hidden in the tool locker and I had drunk half of one of these. It had turned to near vinegar but at least it was fluid. That had been all. Now it was Thursday morning or midday. There had been no water supply in the burning building on the bridge's end. Oh yes, I recalled, I had found two squares of soft chocolate in the pocket of my smock and eaten those. Strangely, I had no appetite – hunger seemed to be taking time off. After the coffee and bread, I fell into a doze again.

It was full daylight now – was it afternoon? A young German soldier, an ordinary *Wehrmacht* man, was shaking me not too roughly by the shoulder. An open military truck had been drawn up outside and into this, together with a number of walking wounded, I was now herded. Beyond being told that we were being taken to a hospital, none of us knew our precise destination. With an armed escort for company, we set off bumpily along the roads of Holland.

The air blowing over my face was refreshing and revitalising, but I couldn't help wondering how long it would be before I enjoyed a ride like this again. Conversation was sparse and I managed to remain taciturn without appearing obviously unsociable. Not a single person in the truck was known to me and I wanted to relax the 'bomb happy' act until we made our next stop. The German soldiers must have felt a certain sense of pride in driving through the streets with their captives, but beyond a casual glance now and again, no Dutch civilian gave us a second look. Only once on the journey did any of us become animated and that was when we spotted two *Gestapo* men in their black uniforms, jackboots and red armbands with white disc and red swastika, strolling side by side along the pavement. There was something indefinably but grossly offensive about their gait and appearance and all of us would, given the chance, have cheerfully torn them limb from limb. Our guards must have sensed something of what was passing through our minds and stiffened into alertness but the moment passed and our anger cooled as we drove on.

I think in some ways I must have been genuinely affected by exhaustion or something similar, for I recall being indifferent to the time of day and the circumstances that we were in. The drive took on the quality of a perfectly normal trip across country and it came as something of a shock to remember where we were and what we were doing when we finally reached our destination. It turned out to be Queen Wilhelmina's summer palace at Apeldoorn.

The great palace had been commandeered as a hospital by the German forces and huge red crosses on white backgrounds had been painted on the roofs. So, for that matter, had they been painted on the roofs of a variety of visiting staff cars, which were clearly anything but ambulances, but '*sauve qui peut*', the prowling rocket-firing Typhoons of the RAF had turned German transportation movements into a nightmare of near certain sudden death. On reflection, I suppose that we were extremely lucky to have reached Apeldoorn unmolested, for our truck had borne no protective insignia whatever but a small red cross flag, most certainly not definable above a height of a few hundred feet.

A somewhat elderly gentleman MO came out to survey his latest intake of patients, but of course, to the twenty-year-old, anyone much over the age of thirty-five appears to be on the brink of senility. I heard him inquire of our driver what nationality we might be.

'*Was sind sie dann? Französisch? Polak?* What are they then, French? Polish?'

'*Englander,*' came the reply.

'*Ach du lieber Gott!*' sighed the MO 'Oh my dear God!' Not the English!'

It was as though he had received one tiresome nationality after another and now, as the final blow in a series of assaults on his equanimity, the English had been sent him as a crowning doom!

'*Holen sie herein,*' he groaned with weary resignation. 'Wheel them inside.'

I picked up the act again and shambled with glazed eyes through the entrance, provoking one or two protests from those I collided with.

Somewhere about this time I was reunited with Captain Simpson. I can only explain this vagueness of recall as being due to the fact that I was deeply preoccupied with the role I was acting out. There must have been times when, unconscientiously, I became so absorbed with staying 'inside the skin of the part' that I had neither eyes nor ears for much else that was going on. Even only weeks after these events there were gaps in my memory that I was completely unable to fill.

We filed along several corridors until we reached what seemed to be a waiting room austerely furnished with hard chairs and a single small table. Simpson acted as interpreter. Either the Germans were ignorant of his rank or chose for some reason to ignore it. We were ordered to strip and all our uniforms were taken away. Some sat, some stood, all of us stark naked.

Fully clothed, Simpson had always projected an elegant, almost debonair image, which he conveyed more by posture and movement than by the clothes he wore. Psychologists today suggest that to remove a man's trousers reduces his self-esteem and can even demoralise or humiliate him. On Simpson, the removal of every stitch of clothing had absolutely no effect whatsoever. The elegant stance, the authoritative tilt of the head, the commanding gestures of hand and arm, and the near eighteenth century panache, all were totally unimpaired. Nor was this bearing and demeanour of his in any way contrived; it was as natural to him as the hair on his head, implanted there by his genes. Yet he was a man gifted with sensitivity and a highly developed sense of humour. Otherwise he would have been intolerable.

High up on one wall was fixed a small loudspeaker about the size of a tennis-ball box. From time to time it crackled and at last began to emit scratchy gasps of music. This box led to my first encounter with Arni, the German medical orderly we were to see so much of over the next few weeks. Somewhere in another room an unseen hand at last succeeded in tuning the master radio and now the music was clearly recognisable as Liszt's Hungarian Rhapsody, one of the only two classical gramophone records in the sergeants' mess at Brize-Norton, which I had come to know by heart

'Ah – Franz Liszt!' I exclaimed, momentarily forgetting my role.

'Brahms!' exploded Arni, with such vehemence that all conversation ceased abruptly. The rousing crescendos continued to pound out from the loudspeaker.

'Er, I'm sure it's Liszt,' I ventured politely. 'We've got the gramophone record.'

'It's Brahms!' insisted Arni. 'Johannes Brahms. *Brahms!*'

Clearly it was a matter of some importance to him. 'Oh, very well,' I conceded, 'If you say it's Brahms, it's Brahms.'

'Of course it is Brahms!' he roared.

This exchange of views was interrupted by the appearance of a second medical orderly whom we later christened 'Weasel'. Small of stature with a long, narrow nose topped by nervous, darting eyes, he shuffled obsequiously into the room bearing a tin washbasin in the manner of a serf at a banquet. Reverentially, he placed the basin on the table and whispered confidentially to Simpson. Simpson's brow arched. Weasel gestured. Finally, Simpson nodded. With superb disdain and massive disgust, he poised himself like a Shakespearean actor. 'He wants us to wash our bollocks in it,' he declared.

Had he been playing for laughs he could scarcely have succeeded better. Every man in the room except the German orderlies was instantly convulsed with uncontrollable belly-laughter. Arni and Weasel were at first bewildered but as they saw us comply one by one, they grew mollified. After all, were not the British mad? And here, if needed, was but further confirmation of the fact. Having completed our anti-louse routine we were next ushered along more corridors to a large communal shower. It was not without misgivings that we filed into this cage work of water pipes. Most of us had read the reports of concentration camp victims being led unsuspectingly into such shower rooms, only to be locked in with deadly cyanide gas. However, such was mercifully not to be our fate. We washed as best we could with soft, brown ointment-like soap, dried and returned to our waiting room. There we experienced another misgiving in that the pyjamas now issued for our wear were of the blue and white striped variety, again, all too familiar in concentration camps. These we donned somewhat reluctantly, supposing them to be the equivalent of British 'Hospital Blues', and were then escorted upstairs to the wards. At this stage, we recovered our footwear.

The upper floor allotted to us consisted of a large open hall or salon with a number of rooms opening off it. All round the walls of this salon were hung rows of watercolours, each one meticulously labelled with a reference number. Old-fashioned canvas fire hoses with brass nozzles were coiled at strategic points, a wise precaution, for a great deal of the palace was constructed of timber. Opposite the entrance to the salon a large expanse of window afforded a commanding view of the forecourt and faced out over a long, tree-lined avenue down which we could see several hundred yards. We were to spend a great deal of time at this window, using the sill as a worktop on which to rewind yards and yards of crepe paper bandages. It also provided our only visual contact with the comings and goings of life 'beyond the bars' and brought home to us the growing realisation of our status as prisoners. It was in every sense our only window on the world and a reminder that, whatever our lot, other human beings were going about their daily lives in comparative freedom within the restrictions imposed by an occupying regime.

To the left and right of this window, doors opened off the salon into smaller rooms allocated as wards. A small room furnished with conventional metal beds was set aside for some officers and no further attempt at segregation was offered. In the larger, adjoining room, two-tier wooden bunks with paillasses had been set up for other ranks. Across the salon, the larger of the two rooms provided only mattresses on the floor and in the smaller, reputed to be Princess Juliana's bedroom, stood more wooden bunks. I spent the first night in the latter and so have ever since been able to boast to friends from Holland that I have done what no Dutchman can lay claim to, namely sleeping in Princess Juliana's bedroom! I can recall the room with its high ceiling decorated with Botticelli-style paintings. It was a lofty room clinging to what remained of its serenity, despite the indignities inflicted upon it, so that whenever I entered I could not shake off the sensation of invading a living, unseen but tangible privacy. Yes Princess Juliana, I may have slept in your bedroom, but with respect. After that, I moved to a mattress on the floor of the larger room.

About this time, I learnt the diagnosis that I had been labelled with but never saw it written and so am unable to spell it. It was '*Commotio*', or was it '*Komozio*'? I do not know to this day but the sound of the word seemed to imply commotion, a disturbance of the mind or brain. That being so, every Airborne soldier there must have been similarly afflicted to a greater or lesser degree. A friend of mine, Bert Parsons, who was in a downstairs ward and of whose presence I was unaware of at the time, told me recently that his recollections of his stay in the palace had always been hazy. He had been wounded in the legs at Oosterbeek, where fighting had continued without respite for ten nights and days, and had been in action for over a week before he was hit. 'I suppose,' he said speculatively, 'not being fully aware of what was going on might have had something to do with not having any food or sleep for eight days.' His words are eloquent enough. To comment on them would be presumptuous.

At all events, the word '*Commotio*', however spelt, seemed to act like a magic charm. When spoken it brought worried frowns to the brows of German medical orderlies and caused them to utter words of concern and sympathy. 'Oh – *Commotio*' they would repeat, almost in awe, '*Commotio*! Then you must lie flat. Very, very flat for two, maybe three weeks. Very flat!' Captain Simpson had, it transpired, done his homework and excelled himself in relating a totally fictitious account of the circumstances leading to my supposed condition. He had described how a mortar bomb had landed in my slit trench. Such had been the force of the explosion that I had been lifted clear into the air and flung a distance of at least five yards to where I had landed, stunned, insensible and seemingly dead. Indeed it was nothing short of a miracle that I was still alive. When feeble movements had revealed that there was still a spark of life left in me, I had been dragged, gibbering no doubt, to a place of comparative safety where, to the astonishment of all, not one single wound could be discerned. The German medical staff were visibly impressed and their concern and sympathy were quite genuine. I really did feel an abominable hypocrite.

A Doctor Schamer was the German MO most of us came to know, like and respect. He had, I learnt, read medicine at Heidelberg and was now in charge of an appallingly ill-equipped surgery-cum-operating theatre. Paper dressings and paper bandages were the order of the day and the latter were always carefully rewound and used again and again until they quite literally came to pieces. The standard application for any type of wound was coal tar ointment and the smell of this blackish unguent seemed to have penetrated the very pores of the building.

The centrepiece of what, I suppose, had served the palace as an elegant reception room, was an operating table resembling a dentist's chair. Onto this contraption British and German wounded were dumped alike without ceremony and in some cases had to be strapped down. So short staffed were the German medical team that anyone entering as a walking patient would almost inevitably be press-ganged into the role of medical orderly. It was here that I had to report for my 'Traubenzucker' or glucose injections, one of the all too few medicaments that were not in short supply and after some days I found myself entrusted with various tasks to carry out at Schamer's behest.

One of these was to assist at an operation on a young Scottish paratrooper. To say that he was young may sound patronising, seeing that I myself had only just turned twenty, but there was something about his flyweight stature and childlike looks that exuded a quality of extreme youthfulness. He was evidently suffering from excruciating pain from a shrapnel wound in his left shoulder. The diminutive X-ray apparatus available to Schamer produced photographs not much bigger than two postcards placed side by side, and these showed that a chunk of metal about the size of a walnut had penetrated Jock's shoulder laterally and was lodged roughly where the humerus meets the end of the collar bone.

Even under chloroform, Jock had to be held down while Schamer deftly removed the shrapnel and packed the wound from his rapidly diminishing stock of surgical gauze. I was given a number of morphine capsules from a British first-aid pack and told to administer them sparingly only when Jock was clearly suffering from acute pain. There was, I was warned, a strong risk of morphine addiction developing if the injections were given too frequently.

The next twenty-four hours were a time of dreadful torment for this courageous little Scot, and during that time, he received no fewer than four injections. Mindful of Schamer's warning, I withheld the morphine for as long as I could bear to, but Jock's greying face, gathering tears and pleadings were too much for me.

It was heartbreaking to see a human being's courage and dignity being sapped in this way, and I was sick to find myself the unwilling instrument of his suffering. Finally, I approached Arni, the senior German medical orderly who, aware of Schamer's overloaded schedule, at first resisted but eventually consented to my request that Jock should have a further examination, after which Schamer arranged for Jock to be shipped off to another hospital nearby where there was a larger X-ray machine.

A day or two later our worst fears were realised. 'Your friend,' explained Schamer, 'died, I am sorry to say, on the operating table.' It transpired that the larger X-ray machine had revealed a smaller piece of shrapnel, further in and sitting almost on the subclavian artery. When the surgeons tried to apply clips to the artery, it had become so deteriorated through local infection that it could not withstand the pressure of the clips and so ruptured. The resulting haemorrhage proved fatal and like Donne's mainland, we became the less. To this day, I have never been able to quite rid my conscience of the feeling that I contributed in some measure to this needless and unwanted tragedy.

There were, however, lighter moments. A Lance Corporal of the Airborne Military Police had been brought in wounded severely enough in both legs to make him temporarily bedridden. By his accents and the slowness of his speech, he must have been a Cotswold man, and although as young as any of us, he bore himself with the demeanour of late middle age. With his bright red hair and placid features, he lay with seeming unconcern day after day, saying little, observing much and puffing occasionally at one of his two pipes, which he had somehow contrived to salvage from the carnage of the battlefield.

The German pre-occupation with rules and regulations is too well known to need exposition here, and one of the hospital rules forbade smoking after nine o'clock at night. The long and short of it was that the Lance Corporal was caught taking an illicit puff considerably after 'lights out'. By this time I had moved into the adjoining ward and heard, but alas did not witness, the ensuing hubbub.

A medical orderly on a routine night-round had evidently sniffed out a telltale whiff of smouldering shag and promptly switched on the lights. A minor pandemonium followed and I could hear German words such as '*rauchen*' (smoke), '*verboten*' (forbidden) and '*strafbar*' (punishable) being yelped in a high major key, accompanied by more mundane British shouts of 'Fuck off', 'Piss off' and 'For fuck's sake let's get back to bloody sleep!' Possibly incensed by the British reaction, the orderly marched out of the ward, holding the two pipes in front of him like stunted wands of office, and returned minutes later with Arni and the Weasel, presumably to act as witnesses. A second altercation flared up, again with British and Germans shouting in antiphony and it became clear that the Lance Corporal was to be duly charged, tried and sentenced the next morning.

The sequel to these events reached such an absurd level of comedy as to be scarcely credible. The standard penalty for smoking after nine o'clock turned out to be three days in the 'cooler', and this the Germans now set about putting into practice. In spite of the desperate fuel economies forced on the Axis powers, an ambulance was summoned, the Lance Corporal was placed with all due care on a stretcher and finally carted off to a local gaol. There he received precisely the same treatment and rations as in the hospital, and three days later, to our enormous relief, he and his pipes were back in our midst.

'What did you make of the experience?' somebody asked him.

The Lance Corporal, like most of the Cotswold breed, was a man of few words.

'I reckon they Germans be proper daft,' he replied, and carried on smoking his pipe.

But now for plans for my own and others' escapes were beginning to take more definite shape, and the proverbial butterflies were starting to make their presence felt in my stomach.

CHAPTER 2

Early Life

With two possible exceptions, nothing in my earlier life had prepared me for the frightening prospects, which now swam like dark and menacing fish through the gloomy waters of my overactive imagination. Brought up in a country vicarage at Shipton-Under-Wychwood, Oxfordshire, I had led what some may call a sheltered and others a privileged life. Like my brother, six years older, and my sister, three years older than myself, I received my early education from a succession of governesses. Beyond the vicarage lawn and garden lay a world as remote and unknown to me as 'Wild Wood' in *The Wind in The Willows*, a favourite book of mine to this day. My father taught me Latin and some rudiments of Greek and coached me at cricket, his favourite game, for he was an MCC member and had captained the university team at Durham, where he had read classics and theology. The church took up a great deal of our time and I sang in the choir or served at communion services. Considered too young to leave home until the age of nine, I was then packed off to boarding school on the south coast, where I suffered agonising pangs of homesickness and, for at least the first three weeks of every term, cried myself to sleep every night. 'Blubbing' it was known as, an unmistakeable symptom of moral turpitude and cowardice of the basest kind and therefore I only dared to give vent to my feelings under cover of darkness and the bedclothes. The school had all the attractions of a junior gaol and, looking back on those days, I see myself then already an embryo prisoner of war. Two years later I was sent to Summer Fields, near Oxford, where I was also a border.

Because of the difference in our ages I was actually dubbed 'too young' to join my brother's or sister's pursuits and so was frequently thrown back on my own resources when it came to entertaining myself. To a child who had by now taken to roaming the fields and hedgerows near my home, my greatest ambition then being to see an otter and spending hours by the River Evenlode watching water rats and making futile attempts to catch fish, the feeling of incarceration in boarding school was barely tolerable. My world was the world of Kenneth Grahame and Henry Williamson and my ideal companions of dream days were Tarka, Salar the Salmon, Mole, Rat, Badger, Otter and Toad. It is a wonder that I ever got any work done at all and what I did, I feel I owe solely to the extreme severity of the regime and the tireless persistence of the masters. Games I took to vigorously, spurred on by the unworthy motive that I might thereby earn the admiration and respect of my schoolfellows and possibly even that of the staff. Cricket was no exception. I played that because I wanted to please my father, who, whatever he taught, always managed to make it tremendous fun. There was, however, one strictly non-curricular activity I found which stimulated a sufficient degree of inward terror to rate as 'adventure' while at the same time providing its own peculiar material and spiritual rewards. I took to breaking school bounds, in order to smuggle in supplies of chocolate, sweets and much coveted Mars Bars.

To do this successfully, a number of factors had to be considered. The timing of each operation was more or less dictated by the school timetable, for absenteeism from either classroom or compulsory games was out of the question and so were Sundays when the shops were shut. As far as I recall, there were only two days a week on which one could rely on being free from games but there were other fortuitous opportunities that presented themselves, such as bonus half holidays or regular half holidays when one was not taking part in a match.

Then there was the question of the route. Summer Fields

possessed over two hundred acres of playing fields and pastureland adjoining the school farm, over much of which was laid a nine-hole golf course. Through the pastureland ran a public footpath from Marston Ferry Road to the south as far as Lonsdale Road to the north. This path emerged in Lonsdale Road from a dark and narrow lane by way of a stile. Within this rural setting, hiding places and all kinds of cover abounded. It was not unusual for a boy to knock a golf ball about with an iron in these meadows and so it was a comparatively simple matter to work one's way round the field as far as the entrance to the Lonsdale Road lane. Once there, a swift check to make sure that one was not observed was all that was necessary and then it was up and over the stile with a golf ball in the pocket and the iron concealed in the hedge. If challenged on the way out, the answer would be simple: 'I sliced a ball down here by mistake sir and thought it might have gone into the road.' And if challenged on the way back: 'I've just been to collect a ball that I sliced down here by mistake sir.' I was always lucky enough, however, to get out and in without being challenged.

The next step involved 'urban tactics'. I was fairly confident that the masters would seldom, if ever, appear in Lonsdale Road because I took it for granted that they would always use the quickest and most direct route to Summertown, as they did on their visits to the Dewdrop Inn. Nevertheless, I was always vigilantly prepared to take instant cover in anyone's front garden and hope to remain undetected until 'the enemy' had passed by. Once at the junction of Lonsdale Road and Banbury Road, careful reconnaissance was needed to assure me that none of the school staff were out on shopping expeditions of their own. Thereafter, it was a matter of a swift but not too hurried approach to the sweetshop and then a return by the same route.

Although I was never caught on these missions, the fear of capture was horribly real and ever present. The penalty would most certainly have been a severe beating and possibly, most dreaded of all, expulsion from the school 'under a cloud'. The embryo prisoner of war was perhaps developing into the embryonic escapee but could the child of Lonsdale Road adventure develop into the youth who would have to face the fear, not only of capture but also the possibility of the firing squad?

CHAPTER 3

A Train to Germany

Our Senior British Officer at the palace was Major Coke of the King's Own Scottish Borderers, whose regiment had contributed a battalion of glider-borne infantry to the strength of the 1st Airborne Division. One of Major Coke's many self-appointed tasks was the collection and dissemination of reliable news items and it was through his jungle telegraph system that we learnt one morning that four of our number had made a successful getaway during the night. Details of their escape were rightly and properly withheld on the well-known 'need to know' principle that no one can part with information that he does not possess. The news, as can be imagined, came as a tremendous boost to general morale which, although never low at any time, was all the better for an occasional fillip to give it a shot in the arm.

The role of those left behind was to conceal the absence of the escapees for as long as possible by means of sheer mendacity and well simulated ignorance. A Captain and three other ranks had escaped and regretfully I cannot recall their names because they came from units other than my own and so were all total strangers. However, '*Ad Unum Omnes*' (All for one, one for all) is the motto of the Airborne Forces and the spirit of that motto now came to life.

'Where is Captain So and So?' A German orderly, after a fruitless search of our upper floor wards, was making a simple appeal for assistance.

'Gone downstairs for treatment,' came an anonymous reply.

'No he has not, that is why I am here.'

'I think he is having a shave,' suggested another voice.

'He is late, tell him he is to come at once when he is finished.'

The orderly tut-tutted his way out through the main doors.

Perhaps half an hour later, another orderly appeared.

'Where is Corporal So and So?'

'Having a Tom Tit.'

'A what?'

'In the toilet mate, we'll send him down for you.'

There followed another tut-tutting exit and so the game wore on. Our friends were all 'in latrines', 'having shaves', 'had gone down to draw the kitchen rations', 'were receiving treatment downstairs', 'had last been seen going downstairs to collect dressings' and so on until at last ingenuity was exhausted. We managed to spin the farce out until shortly after noon, if I remember correctly, which must have gained at least a twelve-hour start before any searches could be organised. It then became abundantly clear that, wherever our friends might be, they were certainly no longer guests of the German Army and we were now treated to a singular display of hysterical Teutonic rage. Arni marched into our midst, followed by the Weasel and several other orderlies, all wearing looks of mingled bewilderment and dismay. It was more than probable that they had already suffered the brunt of his wrath, for Arni's face, still suffused with red, was beginning to regain its natural colour, although a single large vein on his forehead stood out in throbbing, blue relief as his voice rose to the level of a strident Hitlerian rant.

'So!' His words seemed to be involuntarily expelled, as though an unseen hand were inflicting a series of sharp painful blows to the pit of his stomach.

'Four of your men are missing!'

All of us did our level best to register convincing expressions of consternation and disbelief.

'Cor, blimey!' ''kin hell...' 'Well I'm buggered....'

'Silence!' shrieked Arni. 'You will be punished!'

He paused to draw breath and we waited to hear our sentence...

'Altogether!' he continued. 'One by one!'

The British sense of humour, defying precise definition as it does, is variously throughout the rest of Europe derided, misunderstood, shrugged off or dismissed as being merely absurd or puerile. On this occasion it manifested itself as a rapid recognition of the absurd and provoked speechless exasperation. Even severe cases laughed until their wounds must have caused them acute agony and the peals of mirth that rang around the wards would surely have raised the roof of the Collosseum. Rich though the English language may be, flabbergasted must be the only word to describe the reaction of Arni and his colleagues. Their mouths agape with incredulity and indignation, they stared about them for a few moments and then turned about and marched out, with the air of outraged matrons who have unwittingly entered the portals of a Paris brothel. Few of us, I think, can have laughed as much before or since but the sequel was inevitably mundane. Our punishment consisted of a reduction in the Dutch Red Cross cigarette ration from ten down to seven cigarettes daily and the cancelling of our exercise walks in the magnificent palace grounds.

These walks were usually conducted by the Weasel, accompanied by one or more of our teenage German guards. Dressed in ill-fitting greyish uniforms and ankle boots, armed with old fashioned bolt-action rifles, they looked, with their chubby faces that had clearly never seen a razor, like schoolboys at a fancy-dress ball. They could scarcely have been more than fifteen or sixteen years old at the most and seemed bashful and embarrassed by the role that they were called upon to undertake. They had evidently been instructed in some rudiments of propaganda, for occasionally they trotted out stumbling phrases such as 'English pilot good – American nigger pilot bomb Red Cross' or 'England, Germany must fight together Bolshevik' but for the most part our guards were a fairly good-natured lot and if the relationship between us and them was an uneasy one, I never knew it to be unfriendly.

Autumn was beginning now to send out her heralds. There

was crispness in the air, the first tinges of yellow were appearing on the leaves and, here and there, fairy tale toadstools were springing up, red topped with white polka dots, of a kind that I had seen previously only in childhood picture books. There were edible chestnuts too for the gathering and here the Weasel behaved like a projected image of his nickname. He scampered about among the fallen chestnut leaves like a small rodent, flicking and searching with swift paw-like movements of his hands and now and again coming up with a prize, which he would display to us with a crinkled smile of delight gleaming in his little button eyes. He was a not unlikeable weasel and more tolerant than we knew at the time, for it was not until long afterwards that I discovered that the German word for weasel is '*Wiesel*', pronounced 'Veezel', and there can be no doubt that he recognised his nickname and accepted it in good humour.

Strolling, limping or hobbling through these grounds, the sense of serenity was such that, at times, the recollection that a war was in progress could, and often did, come as a sudden jolt. The dignity of sward and woodland remained unimpaired. The lake shimmered tranquil in the weakening sunlight and the dogs and horses of the Dutch Royal family, old companions from bygone days, lay at rest in their respective graveyards, each with a headstone inscribed with tokens of affection and the sadness of bereavement. Not many hundreds of yards distant, we could make out the buildings of the farm, which served the palace. An occasional wisp of chimney smoke told us that life, in some form, was at least surviving there. Beyond the boundaries of this Arcadian parkland lay the realms of speculation, where unseen people lived and worked and fought and died, while we pursued our rambles in an ambience no whit less sequestered than the vicarage gardens of my childhood. Affronted by reminders of our true circumstances, it was difficult to resist a feeling of indignation, as though each such reminder were an outrage against the peace of these sylvan interludes.

Sometimes a troop of German Pioneers, picks and shovels aslant their shoulders, came trampling down the avenue, singing as they marched, so that one might be excused for wondering for a moment whether the Seven Dwarfs had not at last grown up, multiplied and prospered. Occasionally, like the Lady of Shalott we watched them from our window. At other times, we heard them from the grounds. I never heard them sing any other song but one, a sentimental idyll, dredged up, I believe, from the old Kaiser days and dwelling, inevitably on Victory, The Fatherland and Home.

Gloria! Gloria! Gloria Victoria!
Mit Herz und Hand,
Ja, mit Herz und Hand,
Fur's Va-ter-Land!

Glory be! Glory be! Glory be to victory!
With heart and hand
Yes, with heart and hand
For Fatherland!

Whenever they came to the last word of a verse or stanza, they snapped off the final syllable like a broken twig so that it emerged as a kind of yelp, unlike traditional singers who tend to prolong the last note. I suppose to sing it otherwise might have thrown them out of step. Then it was heigh-ho and on to the sentimental bit:

Die Vogelein
Im Walde
Sie sangen
So wunder-wunderschon!

In der Heimat, in der Heimat
Da gibt's ein Wiedersehn,
Ein Wiedersehn
In der Heimat, in der Heimat,
Da gibt's ein Wieder-SEHN!

The songbirds
In the woodlands
They sang
Such a lovely, lovely tune!

In the homeland, in the homeland
We all shall welcome be,
Welcome be
In the homeland, in the homeland
We all shall welcome BE!

On the final syllable, once again, their mouths clamped shut, as though their teeth had suddenly received an order to halt.

Other reminders were less trivial; from time to time we heard, in the distance, unexplained bursts of automatic small-arms fire. There was, at that time, no fighting in Apeldoorn, situated, as it was, a good many miles behind the front line. The Germans, if approached on the subject, simply shrugged their shoulders and would offer no explanation.

Then came a day when the firing was heavier and more prolonged than any we had heard before from the direction of the township. This time it persisted so long that no German staff could pretend not to have heard it. Pressed for an explanation, they finally suggested that it was most probably training or practice, firing at targets. We learnt the true explanation many days later, from the Underground.

Our informant reported that the German occupation authorities had posted notices around the town, ordering all Dutch males between the ages of sixteen and sixty to report for duty at a spot in the town centre by a certain hour in the morning. The work to be carried out was said to be digging trenches or assisting in the building of other defences, and those in possession of bicycles were ordered to bring them, since other transport would not be available. To an uninformed outsider, such a notice might sound innocent enough, were it not for the final paragraph, which warned that failure to comply with the order would incur the usual penalty or statutory punishment, or words to that effect.

The average Dutchman was too old a trout to be caught on a lure of that kind and, as the material time drew nearer, took pains to make himself and his bicycle as scarce as possible. Too many citizens had been spirited away to so-called labour camps, and by 1944, with an end to the war a realistic possibility, determination to survive had become heightened. As for the bicycles, the number of these already appropriated by all ranks of the retreating German forces would, one would have thought, depleted the entire national stock of the Netherlands, but the supply, though dwindling, seemed never quite to dry up. No Dutchman, therefore, was deluded by the naïve implication that defence workers would find their bicycles useful to get about on when moving from site to site.

Accordingly, the Germans now resorted to their, by now, well established methods. They dispatched patrols of SS troops to search homes and round up a representative number of Dutch males. Exactly how many were caught in this particular drive, I cannot say; our informant put the number somewhere between twelve and twenty. These sacrificial victims, who must have known that they were doomed from the moment that they were taken, were then lined up at the assembly point designated by the notice and shot down in cold blood by their SS captors. A further notice, announcing that this was the punishment to be expected for disobeying orders, was placed in a conspicuous position beside the bodies and an armed guard was posted to be sure that no body would be removed prematurely or the notice damaged, defaced or stolen. Truly, as our German orderlies had suggested, there had been firing at targets. That the targets were alive at the time they had apparently thought not worthy of mention.

More reassuring reminders, and majestic in their unhurried progress across the skies, were the gigantic formations of American Fortresses and Liberators, which, on a few occasions, thundered and throbbed on their way towards targets in the hinterland of Germany. In broad daylight and cloudless sunshine, their high altitude making it seem as though they were sauntering, they flew on relentlessly, the sunlight winking and flashing on silvery wing and fuselage like the sudden glint of fish turning in a sunlit stream. Over Apeldoorn they passed unmolested, while neighbouring flak guns squatted in silence, as though their crews were crouching in their burrows like rabbits overshadowed by a falcon's wings. At such times we could not help hoping fervently that the large red crosses painted on the palace roof were big enough to be discerned from high altitude and our German guards openly admitted to genuine terror of heavy bombardment from the air, a feeling which I must confess did not go entirely unshared. Such sights, however, now that our walks had been cancelled, were limited to glimpses through the windows and our outside world was made thus more remote.

As a further measure following the escape of our friends, the Germans now set about categorising our number into two groups, the walking-wounded and those obviously too disabled to move too far from their beds without assistance. It was pretty clear that they were out to separate sheep from goats with the intention of transferring potential escapees to more secure surroundings or direct to *Stalags* or *Oflags*. To this end they laid on a medical inspection of each patient, at the same time administering what seemed to be a massive anti-tetanus injection into the buttocks of every wounded man. My heart sank as I saw the little procession nearing my ward, for I felt now that my little game was up and reflected bitterly that I had missed my chance through sheer procrastination and tardiness in summoning sufficient courage to insist on making an earlier bid. '*Ceux qui hesitant sont perdus*' I remembered and blamed the incipient failure on the cowardice, which I was convinced had taken root in my weakly little soul. If the saying is true that the coward dies a thousand deaths, then I must qualify for the category of 'Super Coward', for I cannot enumerate the countless fears, doubts and pessimistic speculations that played a merry havoc in my mind. While I was brooding in this sickly mood of self-castigation, however, I still managed to observe, with fascination, the bizarre skill of the junior surgeon in charge of the injections. He was followed by an orderly carrying, on a tray, the supplies of serum and two of the largest syringes I have ever seen. They must have been at least the size of a modern tube of 'Smarties' and the hypodermic needles projecting from them were up to four or five inches long. The ritual as each patient was examined was simple. A middle aged medical officer with an experienced and kindly manner asked each man the same question.

'*Wo sind Sie verwundet?*' (Where are you wounded?)

The patient would then display his wound and the doctor would look, nod, hum and ha and murmur in that professional undertone known to hospital patients the world over. While the notes were being written up, the junior surgeon would step forward, armed with the hypodermic needle, which he held in his hand like a darts player, and with the swift flick of a darts player's wrist, would deliver the needle like a missile into the buttock presented to him. Men thus injected hardly flinched but jumped slightly and the needle was almost immediately withdrawn as swiftly as it had been plunged in. Later I discussed these injections with several men and one and all confirmed that they had felt no pain, only a slight thump like someone delivering a playful pat.

My own condition, however, demanded no such treatment and now it was my turn to take part in the rites.

'*Wo sind Sie verwundet?*'

I knew that I should have to answer truthfully and that little hope was left of deluding the searching eyes of this highly professional team. Just the same, more in forlorn hope than in a positive effort to succeed, I had begun to develop a fit of tremors, not too coarse, while the team was working its way in my direction and I will not deny that these tremors assisted greatly in concealing my genuine apprehension of the ordeal I was certain that I must now undergo. I had dire forebodings of the reprisals these sincere, kindly and overworked medics would take and of their righteous anger when they discovered they had been hoodwinked. Swallowing, to overcome a dry mouth, I managed to mumble an answer.

'*Ich bin nicht verwundet.*' (I am not wounded.)

'*Nicht verwundet?*' The doctor repeated the words in astonishment. '*Was ist dann los?*' (Then what is the matter?)

I swallowed again. '*Commotio,*' I replied.

There are moments in life when events about one suddenly seem to go into slow motion. I remember the orderly downing his tray and taking one of my arms while the junior surgeon took the other. Together they gently forced and lowered me onto my mattress.

'Now you must lie down,' they said as before. 'You must lie flat, very flat.'

I have seldom heard sweeter words since.

Spared, for the time being, the prospect of immediate confinement in a *Stalag* cage, I had yet to face the departure of the only familiar face in Apeldoorn, my superbly loyal confederate in conspiracy, Captain Simpson, and it was about this time that I first made the acquaintance of Sergeant Pat Mahoney. If I am inaccurate in this detail of time, it is entirely my own fault for letting matters lie for thirty-eight years before recording them on paper. [The author wrote the manuscript in 1982.] Until I met Pat, Simpson was the only person that I could really afford to trust, for all the soldiers were trained to be on the alert, when in POW situations, for the presence of enemy stool pigeons, and apart from Simpson, I had never, even once, met any of the other inmates at the palace.

My earliest recollection of Pat is of our sitting together on the spacious windowsill overlooking the avenue and rewinding paper bandages on a small gadget resembling a miniature mangle. It was Pat, I think, who taught me that cigarettes could be rolled from this crepe paper, provided that it was stretched until it lost its elasticity. We were fastidious enough to choose the cleaner portions and to store them for future use. One day we tried smoking tealeaves as a substitute for our ration of 'shag' but this turned out to be a revolting disaster and the tealeaves ended up, via the window, in the royal forecourt. Exactly what we talked about on these occasions I could never recall, for I was still intent on babbling nonsense and non sequiturs to fortify my role but I have a distinct recollection of Pat explaining the rewinding gadget slowly, deliberately and with enormous patience. He was a glider pilot from 'F' Squadron stationed at RAF Broadwell, the sister airfield to RAF Brize Norton, then the home of my own 'B' Squadron. Since I had never met him before, I was at first reluctant to trust him, lest he might turn out to be a singularly well informed stool pigeon. The irony of that situation was, as I learnt much later, that because of my abnormal demeanour and frequent visits to the downstairs surgery, I was, myself, under suspicion of being a German undercover man. I think Simpson must eventually have put in a word for me before he and other walking-wounded were taken off to the camps. Pat, although wounded in the foot, was able to walk but somehow managed to persuade the authorities that he was unfit enough to remain behind. Simpson, alas, without so much as a scratch on his bandaged ankle, was quickly pronounced fit enough to leave.

There were, however, anomalies and one of these affected another glider pilot whom I had come to know as Bud Brailey. Bud had been badly wounded by a mortar bomb, both in his back and in the backs of his thighs and I believe one of the splinters in his back had penetrated the base of a lung. He could certainly walk but with great pain and was in far worse condition than Pat Mahoney; nevertheless, he had been judged fit to move on. In order to get at his wounds, the medics on the battlefield at Oosterbeek had ripped open his battledress blouse and shirt with scissors and when our uniforms were brought out of stores for the evacuation, both of these garments were in tatters. For Bud to face a long, cold winter in these garments was unthinkable, so I gave him my almost undamaged Airborne smock. I record this now, not as an act of magnanimity, but because of a much, much later sequel, which throws light on the character of Bud Brailey.

It was clear now that the plans to move out the first wave of our number were well advanced. Although it was only a matter of days since we had been taken, the items of personal kit and clothing that reappeared seemed to belong to a remote and distant past. Men sat about on beds turning over their possessions thoughtfully, as though they were contemplating newly acquired purchases and tension began to invade the atmosphere like the vibration of muted strings. The 'Waiting Game' was under way once more.

On the morning scheduled for departure, Pat and I were sitting on our usual windowsill, rewinding bandages. Ambulances would take our men to the station, we had been told, and thereafter a Red Cross train would carry them to their destinations in Germany. Most farewells had been taken, Simpson had thoughtfully introduced me to Major Coke before shaking me by the hand and wishing me luck, ambulances were assembling outside, men were sitting on their beds smoking, or wandering about in the manner of impatient passengers and all seemed set for another routine day of dressings, treatment, meals and the everlasting bandage winding!

The first burst of flak came from out of sight and sounded directly overhead. Within seconds another followed it and another and then all hell broke loose as every flak gun for miles around joined in a furious burst of cannonades. I do not recall hearing a siren; possibly the racket of the gunfire could have drowned it out. Our guards, candidly shaken, begged us to get away from the windows but nothing could have torn us away, transfixed as we were by the matchless display of coolness and courage being enacted before us.

Insouciantly, insolently even, in their scorn of the enemy gunners, four rocket-firing Typhoons of the RAF hove into view, flying in a perfect line-astern formation as though at peacetime Farnborough, with black puffs slowly catching up on their 'Tail End Charlie'. I know that I have never witnessed, before or since, anything in the air to excel the sheer skill and audacity of these pilots. Not a wing tip wavered, not a rudder flickered them out of line; their discipline could have stood as the equal and envy of any British battle line in history. As we watched with a mixture of awe, admiration and fear for their lives, it became clear from the flak bursts that the German gunners were improving on their range and altitude and then we were treated to the most breathtaking feat that I have ever seen. Whether by intuition or judgement, I shall never know, but I suspect by a compound of both, the leader peeled off into a classic sixty-degree dive of attack, followed in turn by the other three; as the last Typhoon pilot flicked into his peel-off, the flak burst in a puff precisely where he had been flying barely a split second before.

Whatever was being attacked in the town was certainly receiving a thorough pounding but trees obscured any hope of our seeing the actual target. The Typhoons were wheeling and, like gannets at sea, suddenly diving out of sight below our tree top horizon, then reappearing as suddenly, zooming upward in steep climbs. With each dive, we could hear the 'whoosh' of rockets and the rattle of cannon fire and, by now, all of the flak guns had gone silent. It is possible that the attack lasted five minutes, it might well have been even less. Then, their task completed, the four aircraft reformed in line astern and flew off, apparently unscathed, southward towards the Allied lines. Years later, I met a Typhoon pilot who had operated over France and Belgium. 'Our orders were simple,' he told me. 'If you see anything moving, stop it and if you see anything stopped, move it!'

Something had most certainly been stopped or moved, or both, in Apeldoorn, for very shortly afterwards Arni and Weasel arrived to tell us that the evacuation of wounded had been postponed and that peculiarly British weapon of derision, the faint and ironic cheer, greeted their announcement. Both Arni and Weasel were plainly put out by this reception, but to do them justice, they were as loyal to their national pride as circumstances could allow and tried to give the impression that the postponement was due to anything but the intervention of the RAF. Transport reorganisation and priorities for other troop movements were vaguely referred to and when pressed for an answer as to what the Typhoons had actually hit, Arni became very irritated and intimated that he didn't see what concern it was of ours anyway. Under further pressure, reluctantly and with rather bad grace, he agreed that he would try to find out. Later, in the manner of an actor throwing away lines, he informed us that the Typhoons had hit 'a pen and ink factory' and brushed aside the topic of the raid as though it had been an act of mindless vandalism. I remained convinced that the Dutch Underground had communicated news of the intended troop movement to their contacts behind the Allied lines and the 'cab-rank' Typhoons of the Tactical Air Force had been briefed to take appropriate action.

Arni remained aloof for just long enough to maintain his dignity and then reverted to his usual genial behaviour. He was a man, as near as I could judge, in his early forties, with sparse grey hair austerely clipped to the minimum length at which it would lie flat. Somewhat short of six feet tall, he kept his figure in good shape and his turnout was always exemplary. Shrewd blue eyes looked out from under punctiliously trimmed eyebrows and his whole manner and bearing bespoke the disciplined soldier, which he undoubtedly was. I think I first became aware of him as a personality, rather than an anonymous enemy soldier, when he was extolling the values of castor oil. According to Arni, this fluid was unrivalled in its versatility and only the very ignorant recognised it solely as a purgative. Far from it! It was an excellent hair tonic and brilliantine and here he displayed his scrupulously groomed, if scant, coiffure; it made a fine lubricant, as witness the smooth-running and soundless bearings of the hospital wheelchairs; finally, it kept one's boots both smart and supple and at this point he proffered his jackboots for inspection, lest by chance there lurked among us a 'Doubting Thomas'. He had a penchant, too, for relating lengthy anecdotes, which, in order that we should not be misled in any way, he invariably prefaced with the declaration 'Now I shall tell you a very funny story!' The only one of these stories that I can recall concerned an elephant and its owner who, for reasons withheld by Arni, were attempting to travel on the Berlin underground railway and the owner was encountering setbacks from every official that he approached. One after another, they refused to sell a ticket for the elephant but none would offer any reason until, at last, one of them relented and explained 'Your elephant cannot have a ticket because it is forbidden on the Berlin Underground to carry *trunks*!' The punch-line was delivered with a staccato burst of ha ha ha, followed by the reminder, lest any should have missed the point, '*That was a very funny story*!' The British audience always responded uproariously to these tales and poor Arni was obviously convinced that his jokes had gone down well. Not one of us ever had the heart to tell him that it was he and not the story that was the sole butt of our laughter. Oh perfide Albion!

By his own account, he had learnt English before the war in South Africa, where he had been involved in coastal trading round various ports on some kind of small cargo vessel. I received the impression that he had not returned to join the *Reich* forces of his own free will, for while he was certainly a correct and loyal soldier, he had seen too much of the world to become a dedicated Nazi. On one occasion he acted as my escort when I was detailed off to help collect some Red Cross parcels from downstairs near the kitchens. As we passed along a stone-flagged corridor, with Arni's boot-heels ringing out at every step, we met face to face with a German Warrant Officer coming the other way. The two Germans stopped for a brief exchange of words about our business in that part of the palace and then '*Heil* Hitler!' barked the WO banging his heels and raising his arm in the Nazi salute. '*Heil* Hitler!' barked Arni, following suit and blushed scarlet to the roots of his hair. Neither of us spoke but he knew I had seen and sensed his embarrassment.

One day I revealed to Arni that I had begun to think of reading medicine after the war, although it would have been more truthful to say that my mother had been doing her best to push me into it. I suppose in my callow, adolescent way, I rather fancied myself in the role and with the status of doctor without paying sufficient or any attention to the heavy demands of the work entailed. Nevertheless, I had found sufficient genuine interest to read some of the books my sister had used in her SRN (State Registered Nurse) training at St Thomas' Hospital and had thereby gleaned a patchy knowledge of human anatomy and physiology. In addition, like many soldiers, I had attended first aid classes and so could be rated not entirely useless as an apprentice ward orderly. Arni duly reported my limited potential to Dr Schamer, who began to add to my tasks in his surgery and showed a fatherly interest by coaching me in various methods and techniques, which he employed in his daily work. My hypocrisy was thus further compounded. From the pupa of the bogus shell shock case was emerging the bogus medic – a metamorphosis that, while it served an end at the time, I recall with absolutely no pride whatsoever.

The brief respite afforded by the Typhoon raid lasted some forty-eight hours and then all doubt about the coming move was dispelled as transport began to assemble again outside. I recollect no touching scenes of farewell; on the contrary, the prevailing spirit was one of genuine cheerfulness. It was as though we were seeing a group of friends off on their holidays and the holidaymakers were responding in like mood. Our sense of loss when they had gone, however, was very present as we speculated with some concern about their immediate future. But gone they were and that was that, if only for the time being, and we who were left had to make the best of it while we could. I can only presume that I was left behind because I had begun to be of some small help to an understaffed and overworked hospital team. Where had all the nurses gone? Back to Germany? Certainly not to the Eastern Front. Our British and Allied nursing sisters were often within range of enemy artillery and frequently worked valiantly in conditions far worse than those in Apeldoorn, where at least there was some shelter and a bed of sorts. I only ever saw one female German nurse, a formidable figure with a ramrod back and a profile like that of Julius Caesar on our school Latin books. Her horn-rimmed spectacles likewise resembled those that schoolboys delight in adding to such profiles. From beneath a stiff white apron and brown cloak protruded legs, button-booted to the knee, which lent her gait a parade-ground quality and I never once saw her turn her eyes from whatever direction that she happened to be heading in. She never came near us, nor we to her. With the British soldier's uncanny knack for coining nicknames, the men christened her 'Hitler's Last Hope'. Elsewhere there were a few '*Flakmädchen*' about, German Army girls who assisted the flak regiments, known by the Dutch as the 'Grey Mice', but who undertook no hospital duties. A few women cleaners and kitchen assistants, former palace employees, had been retained by the Germans, along with some elderly male civilian staff; otherwise the entire hospital was run by male members of the German Army medical corps.

Looking out of our avenue window in a south-easterly direction, one could just make out, through trees and over a wall, the homes and kitchen gardens of the royal servants. The distance to the nearest one was something under a hundred yards and though from our windows we could not discern any entrance to this area, the wall was not high enough to present any serious obstacle to a determined climber. As plans for escape passed through our minds, it became plain that any initial exit would have to be made over that wall, for any attempt to pass unseen down the avenue would be nothing short of foolhardy. Even now, as I write, the fears and misgivings that plagued me when faced with the reality of our project, nearly forty years ago, return as ghostly reminders of past inadequacies. I doubted my ability to carry the project through; I feared that what little courage I could muster would crumble, that I would 'let the side down' in some way and become an object of scorn and ridicule, a social pariah and an outcast, the man whose guts had failed him when put to the test. I think I feared shame and opprobrium more than anything. As for the fear of pain and sudden death, I deliberately blinded myself to such possibilities, for to contemplate them brought on an acute physical and mental torment akin to nausea

– 'sick with fear' is no idle choice of words. To confide these feelings to anyone in that hospital was unthinkable; the subject of personal apprehensions was strictly taboo and criminally damaging to morale. People like Major Coke, I believed, were born devoid of fear; tough regulars like Pat Mahoney spat on it. Where could I turn, what straws could I clutch at in this ocean of fear, whose every wave-top was flecked with towering panic?

CHAPTER 4

The Glider Pilot Regiment

There had been three occasions in the remote past when I was utterly convinced that death was only moments away and the first of these was in early childhood at the age of about six. It may seem derisory to recall the first incident but none the less, it was horrifyingly earnest at the time. On a sunny day in Shipton churchyard, I had thought to find pleasure for a short time swinging between two gravestones. It was easy enough, for the gravestones stood side by side and, by placing a hand on each in the manner of a gymnast on parallel bars, I was able to enjoy swinging to and fro, increasing the angle of tilt at every backward and forward thrust. I knew, however, that I was doing wrong, for as clergy children we had been strictly brought up to respect and revere the graveyard and its occupants. To borrow the words of an old flying instructor, I then let my enthusiasm overcome my judgement, miscalculated a backward swing, fell flat on my stomach and winded myself. The shock of being winded is never a pleasant sensation and this was my first experience of it. A local farmhand, who was scything the grass nearby, heard my gasps and howls and strolled over to see what was amiss. I managed to gulp out some words to the effect that God had punished me and I was dying, which I honestly believed to be true, but the mower reassured me that I was only winded and returned to his scything without further concern. Nevertheless, to a child of six, the vision of imminent death was terrifyingly real and the memory of it indelible.

My next encounter was more fearsome. As a child of ten at

boarding school on the south coast, I had joined my schoolmates in an early morning run to the beach and dip in the sea. Being then a non-swimmer, I never ventured out of my depth, but on this occasion I was gradually tugged seawards by the undertow. Fully aware of what was happening, I tried to attract attention by shouting but everyone else was shouting happily at the time and my cries went unheard. The waves slowly began to close over my head but in a last and desperate attempt to survive, I allowed myself to sink until my feet touched the bottom, from where I could kick myself violently upwards to break surface. This allowed me sufficient time to wave my arms, shout for help and draw breath for my next descent. In some wretched book, or other, I had read that a drowning man surfaces three times only before he is lost for ever and when I came up for the third time, I had no doubt whatsoever that I was doomed. Eventually, the master in charge of the bathe dragged me none too gently into the shallower water and curtly ordered me to stop fooling about. 'But I wasn't fooling about, sir,' I tried to explain. 'Shut up!' came the reply. In those days, one did as one was told.

By coincidence, the third occurrence also took place at sea. I was staying with a school friend at Bognor Regis and the family owned a small dinghy with an outboard motor. One day, when the rest of the family were otherwise occupied, I decided to try a little voyage on my own. This was unbelievably foolhardy, for I was still a non-swimmer. I must have been about twelve by then and understood more or less how to start the motor with the lanyard and steer the boat. All went well until the motor stopped when I was a couple of hundred yards out. I panicked until I remembered that I had not turned the petrol on and realised that I had covered the distance on what was left in the carburettor. I turned the tap and wrenched and wrenched desperately at the lanyard, all the time being swept further out to sea. I was nearly in tears when the motor finally came to life and, overwhelmed by relief, I moved from the seat amidships to take the tiller in the stern. It was a disastrous move. Up went the bows, down went the stern and water flooded the air intake. Nothing that I knew would start the motor now but I discovered a single oar in the boat. With this, however, I was unable to make any headway and I was appalled by the distance to the shoreline. Moreover, the rollers seemed to be growing bigger and more menacing and the dinghy began to ship water. I did not shout and I did not yell. I simply screamed and screamed for help and mercy, for me it seemed that death was stalking closer with every approaching wave. Such panic, once ungoverned, becomes ungovernable. I was eventually rescued and towed in by a local boatman and suffered torments of shame for days and weeks afterwards.

How then had this pusillanimous little schoolboy, with his record of panic in the face of fear, come to be first a member of The Glider Pilot Regiment, secondly to be involved in the action at Arnhem Bridge and thirdly now to be contemplating a serious attempt at escape through enemy-held territory?

I suppose one of the first steps had been to enter St Edward's School, Oxford, with the aid of a minor scholarship. In the meantime, my father had died when I was eleven years old and still at Summer Fields School. This must seem a very casual reference to the death of a parent but though I did grieve considerably at the time, I had, little by little, ceased to know him except as a somewhat distant figure of authority whom I regarded with some of the fear of the unknown. The cricket coaching of the earlier days had petered out, no more were the Latin lessons and the more I grew, the less I saw of him. Years later, to my immense chagrin, I learnt that because of a premonition of his approaching end, he had deliberately withdrawn from my company. 'I don't want to make too much of a pal of Godfrey,' he had confided to my mother, 'because he would miss me too much when I go and when he most needs me.' Thus, fatherless and dependent on a widowed mother, I entered public school and the third boarding school in my life.

It is neither my wish nor intention to denigrate St Edward's but I cannot truthfully say that I was ever really happy there. Once again, I strongly resented being made to board but the rule dictated that no scholar, however undistinguished, was allowed to be a dayboy. Following my father's death, our family had moved into North Oxford and this made the situation seem all the more unreasonable. Added to that, it was the tradition in those days for all new boys to be treated as less than dirt and I was inwardly furious at the indignities, great and small, that I was obliged to suffer in silence. There were ludicrous taboos and shibboleths to be observed and the 'fagging' system was in full swing. New boys had to button up all three buttons of their jackets, for instance, and hands had to be placed in trouser pockets from behind the jacket tails, not from the front! The list, if continued, would be a wearisome one and it bred within me only a growing indignation. The Head Boys of dayrooms were, for the most part, 'Little Hitlers', house prefects were authorised to administer canings and 'fags' had to answer the fagging bell at the double whenever a prefect wished to rid himself of a distasteful or disagreeable chore. However, to give St Edward's the benefit of the doubt, I suppose that it was going through a bad patch at the time. During the years from 1938 to 1940, most young men worth their salt had volunteered for the armed forces, so that the teaching staff was left drained of little else but older men and young incompetents and, inevitably, I found the teaching uninspiring against the backcloth of the war clouds outside. From time to time, from a classroom window, one could catch glimpses of platoons of infantry in battle-order and steel helmets route marching up the Woodstock Road and the RAF was often overhead. It was with these people that I identified and, growing sick of the hothouse atmosphere of the classroom, I longed to join their ranks as soon as age would allow.

Nevertheless, there were two activities that brought me genuine pleasure and, for these, I proffer St Edward's unstinted and ungrudging thanks. One of these was the OTC (Officer Training Corps), forerunner of today's Army Cadet Corps and, the other, the free use of the RAF section of the school library. The former provided a great sense of satisfaction in being more closely aligned with contemporary world events. I actually enjoyed drill and musketry, developed a keen enthusiasm for shooting on the range and, by the age of sixteen, could strip and reassemble a Bren gun as quickly as our instructor. Field craft, I absorbed as though by nature and mock battle days with blank cartridges were, for me, the highest form of entertainment available. Schoolboy games perhaps but sure beginnings. No one in my immediate family, including grandparents, had ever, to my knowledge, seen military service of any kind and I can only account for this military enthusiasm as being due to the indirect influence of my favourite Uncle Tommy. To me he was a paragon of what I imagined a man should be; a dauntless rugby player, a ferocious fighter when the need arose, a valiant soldier and an honest priest. He had taken Holy Orders after nearly four years in the Great War, during which he had been gassed on the Somme while rescuing his men from their gun emplacements. I needed to look no further for inspiration.

As for the school library, for years, I had cherished a passion for aircraft of every description. I had collected pictures of them, made models of them, read ream after ream of air stories of the Great War and the peak of all my ambitions was to fly a fighter aircraft. Here now in the library, I came across what, to me, was a jewel among the pebbles, *The Royal Air Force Manual of Flying Training*. I roamed in wonder through this El Dorado of delights and derived from it that unvirtuous feeling of superiority in knowing that of which the herd knew not! What did the prefects know, for instance, about airfield circuit procedures and crosswind landings? How pitiful was the ignorance of the Head Boy of the dayroom who knew nothing of stick or rudder bar or the niceties of a three-point landing. How swiftly my housemaster would perish under a dive of attack out of the sun! From these and similar reflections, I drew strength in times of adversity and revelled in countless imaginary flights on dismal days. Again, there had been no fliers in my family; indeed, my mother was implacably opposed to aviation in any form and subscribed to that doctrine which preaches that 'If God had intended man to fly, he would have given him wings.' There was, however, a subversive agent within the family circle in the person of The Reverend

Charles Hann, an ex-Great War fighter pilot. Like my Uncle Tommy, he had taken Holy Orders after the war, during which he had flown and fought in the Sopwiths and SE5s of his day. By the time I had come to know him as an honorary uncle, he had adopted a habitual attire of white dog collar and long black cassock. Once, during my wartime training days on Tiger Moths at EFTS, I ran into Charles Hann on leave and remarked to him that the Tiger was not, in appearance at any rate, unlike the front-line aircraft that he had flown in combat. 'Tell me,' I asked him, 'What were flying conditions like in your day?' Charles Hann favoured me with a broad grin. 'Godfrey, my boy,' he replied, 'When I started flying, I wasn't even a Christian and just look at me now!' Although neither he nor Uncle Tommy could ever replace my father, there is no doubt that they set me a standard to strive for, however unattainable it might seem to be.

I left St Edward's at the age of sixteen. Few clergy are to be found among the higher income groups and, scholarship or no scholarship, our family finances could no longer cope with the expense of my education. Before I left, however, I had developed a further extra-curricular skill as a kind of extension to my smuggling trips at Summer Fields. Resenting, as I did, being incarcerated a mile or so from our new home, I discovered a devious route, which involved crossing the Oxford Canal and working my way through the fields under cover of hedgerows, that would bring me back into the streets via a canal bridge near our house. Ironically, perhaps, the successful negotiation of this route was a by-product of the field craft training that I had received in the OTC. On such occasions, my mother dutifully upbraided me but, like a loyal underground agent, never betrayed the secret to the enemy!

There was now little more than a year to go before I could volunteer for the RAF and I was allowed to follow what, to my astonishment, was rated as a sensible choice. Morris Motors of Cowley had been converted into a CRU (Civilian Repair Unit) and were restoring to active service aircraft damaged in combat or training. The Spitfire, Hurricane and occasional Boulton Paul

Defiant were brought there as battle casualties, while from the training stable came the Miles Magisters and Masters. I felt that if I were one day to fly these aircraft, it would be a distinct advantage to learn something about their construction. In the event, I was to learn a great deal more about the human race, for it was my first encounter with the British 'Working Class'.

To be cocooned in vicarage and boarding school for most of one's life is scarcely an ideal preparation for coping with the greater world outside. The sociologists had not begun to cut their capers in those days, so the class structure was still a relatively primitive concept. There were the 'Aristocrats' who floated in a lofty world somewhere between their grouse moors and the House of Lords, there were the 'Gentry', readily identifiable by their mode of speech, and there was a huge amorphous mass known as the 'Middle Class'. Lastly, there was a shadowy and mysterious community, casually referred to as the 'Working Class'. Most of us have fallen at some time into the common blunder of assessing human beings collectively as groups rather than individually as persons. I fell foul of the same pitfall and viewed the 'Working Class' with secret apprehension. Little by little, sometimes painfully, the layers of prejudice were stripped away and the truth made more discernible. 'The world in all', as Marvell observed, 'doth but two nations bare: The good, the bad and these mixed everywhere.' Seeing that I was to spend the next six years in the ranks, I could have learnt few lessons more valuable.

Of the aircraft, I learnt disappointingly little, for my work was confined to repairing and testing hydraulic fittings and visits to other works departments had to be made furtively and were thus necessarily brief. I drifted out, after six months in the factory, onto a tractor driving instructor's course and went north to teach these newfound skills to Stonyhurst sixth formers. Home Guard activities and working in canteens run by the Church Army or YMCA occupied the rest of my time. It was not a commendable way to live; I was simply marking time until I was old enough to enlist.

The morning of the aircrew medical tests found me in a, by now, fairly familiar state of jitters. 'What if...' questions were darting about in my mind like minnows and I dared not contemplate the possibility of failure. In consequence, the medical board's findings caught me unguarded and barely able to sustain the appalling bitterness of the blow. I had a depressed sternum, they said, and so was rated unfit to fly. The RAF recruiting sergeant was both sympathetic and helpful; he promised to tear up my papers and advised me to try again a fortnight later, when there would be a new medical board. Fate struck again. One doctor from the previous board had remained to join the new one. Mortified and, in a state of utter dejection, I went downstairs to the next floor and volunteered for the Oxfordshire and Buckinghamshire Light Infantry.

'How old are you son?' asked the sergeant. I told him truthfully that I was seventeen and a quarter but was prepared to give my age as eighteen.

'Are we likely,' he inquired, 'to have any trouble from your parents if they find out?'

'Oh no, no' I lied cheerfully, 'none at all, none whatsoever.' He looked thoughtful.

'I'll tell you what I'll do,' he said at last, 'I'll go and have a word with my CO. In the meantime, you take a walk around the block and when you come back, you may find that you are a bit older.'

I did as I was bidden.

Compared with St Edward's School, life at the Cowley Barracks was like a Sunday school treat. There were no idiotic taboos or shibboleths, everywhere was bustle and activity and the regimental organisation was superb.

'Whatever other units you may serve in, son,' the recruiting sergeant had assured me, 'you will always remember your first regiment as your best.'

To this day, I retain a strong sense of family affection for the old OBLI (Oxfordshire and Buckinghamshire Light Infantry), and the eight months I spent with them provided incomparable training for the rigours and deprivations to come. During that period, we witnessed a visit from a demonstration platoon of the 52nd, the first unit to be trained and equipped as an air landing force and my very first sight of the newly forming Airborne Forces. In 1942 in Northern Ireland, a circular came our way, calling for volunteers for a brand new unit, The Glider Pilot Regiment, to carry Airborne Forces into action. With the CO's permission, I was allowed to apply and eventually found myself facing a third aircrew medical board and my very last hope of ever learning to fly. All went well this time, except for a minor contretemps during the hearing test, which was conducted by a somewhat peppery Squadron Leader MO. After listening to his watch ticking at various distances, I was ordered to stand in the far corner of the room and repeat numbers, which he would whisper to me.

'Eighty-seven,' he breathed, or some such number, like a spy passing on a secret message. Infected by his conspiratorial manner, I lowered my voice to an undertone.

'Eighty-seven,' I repeated.

'*Speak up man!*' he roared, 'I can hardly hear you!'

I feared he might fail me on grounds of imbecility but this time my tests were satisfactory and there had been no mention of depressed sternums. It was like a reprieve. I was already at two thousand feet and reaching for the clouds.

CHAPTER 5

Plotting the Escape

There is an old Chinese proverb, which runs 'Fear knocked at the door, Faith opened it and, lo, there was no one there.' So far as I was concerned, fear was certainly knocking at the door at Apeldoorn but I had not heard of the proverb then and did not have the faith to open the door. It had been one thing to make a decision to escape while in high spirits on the end of Arnhem Bridge; it was quite another to sit down and cold bloodedly plot the manner of that escape whilst fully aware of the hazards involved and the very possibly fatal consequences of failure. These doleful reveries had about them a sepulchral quality, as though mocking death's hands in German helmets were beckoning me into their line of fire and I could all but hear their derisive glee as I was inexorably drawn into their dance macabre. Shuddering inwardly at such thoughts, I did my best to present as cheerful a countenance as I could, ever conscious of the extraordinary gift of courage with which Pat Mahoney and Major Coke seemed to be endowed. If they shared my misgivings, they most certainly never spoke of them or revealed them in any way; while added to my other fears was the conviction that sooner or later they would detect the 'yellow streak' that I was at such pains to conceal and banish me from any further participation as a child too young to join in grown up games.

We sat for most meetings round a Monopoly board, a gift from the Dutch Red Cross and a superb cover for clandestine conversations. Full credit for the planning of our mini-operation must go to Major Coke and Pat Mahoney, who, from time to time, exchanged meaningful glances, which I was unable to interpret at the time but which clearly related to some matter of which I had no knowledge. As we rolled the dice and bought or sold properties I was aware of a very watchful quality in Pat's manner and felt myself to be under scrutiny. However, I challenged him on this point and always regarded him as the leading light in the whole affair, though it was unquestionably Major Coke who gave the orders and assumed command of the enterprise. There is also no doubt in my mind that Pat's Irish ancestry constituted a very valuable asset in that he had inherited the quick-witted and intuitive intelligence of the Celts and with it, the ability to profit by tact and persuasion where a simple Anglo-Saxon might have sought bluntly to hammer his points home. During one of our Monopoly sessions it was revealed to me that Pat had, for some time, been acting as a courier between Major Coke and the kitchens and I realised then why he was one of the fatigue party who collected our meals. These meals had to be fetched from below stairs and, while in generous bulk, were of the monotonously institutional fare, which one might in the circumstances expect. Breakfast was always a frugal affair, consisting largely of slices of komisbrot and the inescapable acorn coffee but the noonday meal was more varied, consisting of German sausage or anonymous stews. Once we actually had fresh venison, from a deer shot in the Royal Park, cut meticulously into one-inch cubes and stewed to near disintegration. This particular meal caused some mild amusement at the time for a paratrooper had seen the carcass being carried in at the time and misidentified it as a donkey; once reassured, however, he devoured his meal like the rest of us. With such delicacies, there was usually a vegetable of some kind but, always without fail, there were vast quantities of boiled and mashed potatoes served in the large metal bowls commonly found in Army ablutions. But there was a break with tradition. It is an unwritten rule in the British Army in the field that no officer sits down to a meal until every other rank has been adequately fed; nevertheless, one bowl of potatoes always found its way directly into the room occupied by Major Coke and two or three brother officers and often at the hands of Pat Mahoney. It was a simple but risky form of internal postal service. A written note from the Underground was buried in the potatoes, later to be extracted like a sixpence from a Christmas pudding, by Major Coke or one of those in the know and any reply was returned with the dirty dishes. This line of communication stretched far outside the palace and its Dutch operators were men and women of supreme courage who bore the appalling strains of their self-imposed duty with tenacious and unswerving loyalty. It was by means of their selfless devotion that a carefully planned and co-ordinated escape plan was made a valid possibility but the one thing that we seemed to lack was a map.

Unbeknown to me at the time, Pat had managed to retain his aircrew escape maps but kept them well concealed; they would have been too large, when opened out, to have consulted during our Monopoly sessions. But, by a sheer fluke, I came across a smaller one. The Dutch Red Cross had provided, among other efforts, a selection of books written in English and one of these was a tourist edition of *Wandering in Holland*. A by no means inappropriate title it turned out to be and the frontispiece consisted of a basic map of Holland. Although far from detailed, main towns, roads and rivers were clearly marked; it was, at least, sufficient to orientate by and was easy to conceal under the Monopoly board. Our escape would clearly have to be planned in two phases: first, the immediate getaway from Apeldoorn and, second, the route through open country, which would take us back to Allied lines. It was for the latter phase that the little map was so useful and as we studied it, we discussed the merits and demerits of the various detours open to us. The British and Americans had certainly reached the Lower Rhine but to head for the nearest troops would be to court disaster, for if the Germans were troubling to look for us anywhere, they would expect to find us on a southerly route. North and east were out of the question for we should be heading still deeper into German-occupied territory. We finally agreed that to strike out north-west would give us the best chance, being the nearest to opposite direction to where the enemy would be searching.

Having settled that matter, our next problem was one of clothing. At present we were wearing the prison-style pyjamas with the blue and white stripe; fatal clothing by day or night and so we had to find a substitute. Fortune, however, was on our side; some of the men were issued with khaki, so it was fairly easy to arrange a swap. As for footwear, both Major Coke and I possessed boots while Pat retained his footwear. Major Coke was undeniably fond of his boots and, from time to time, took them out to examine them, though he spent a good deal of his time in bed. He was not seriously hurt but the wound seemed to give him a lot of pain, so he rested it when possible. There was nothing to be seen but two small holes where a bullet had passed through his left thigh, fortunately missing the bone, so we assumed that time alone would heal and make it well again.

Food was now the next consideration. We decided to take a small amount with us from the Red Cross parcels and all of it in tins. The parcels were also a godsend for we used them to tempt our captors, lull them into a false sense of security and, we hoped, lower their guard. We laid on a spread and invited Arni, Weasel and, eventually, Dr Schamer. There were many delicacies that the German Army had not seen for many a day – butter, sugar, tea, jam, biscuits and the like, so we plied our guests with fine fare while we talked of what we could do when the war was over, all wounds were healed and all swords turned back into ploughshares. It was a strange mixture of friendship and hypocrisy for on the one hand our feelings were genuine while on the other we knew perfectly well what we had in mind. Schamer behaved like a perfect gentleman and even Arni seemed more relaxed. One day we found Weasel in tears and enquired, quite kindly, what was the reason? For a long time he refused to answer but finally broke down. He had been posted, he told his interrogator, to the Eastern Front.

I do not recall exactly when, but I do know that we received a dose of advocaat and on another, a cupful or two of mulled red wine. Did all prisoners receive this, I wondered, or were we oddly favoured folk? Certainly no one seemed to be violently opposed to us now. The hospital appeared to run more smoothly, routine became an established rule and lights were extinguished at half past nine in the evening. Then, the devil would strike again!

While half of me was working as a machine, the other half took over at night and worked on fear. I cannot say how long its duration was but it seemed to vary with the last thing that I did at night. At least the night was friendly; I counted that in my favour. It always came regularly and there was no disturbance until the morning. Under my pillow lay a crust of komisbrot, for by now I always scrounged some bread with which to while away the darkening hour. As I chewed, I thought. What were the forces on my side? There was Pat's paternalism but against that, was the unknown person of Major Coke. Would he see through me in the end and finally forbid my exit? Then there were the guards. Supposing one of them turned back, with or without his girlfriend, because of forgetting something or because it had begun to rain? They had been timed for thirty to forty minutes dozens of times and had always stuck in pairs, sometimes with *Flakmädchen*. What if they should suddenly decide to go the opposite way in singles? Well, that one wasn't too bad. We should notice it and just have to wait, I supposed, or revise our plan. How about other guards or other troops? Time would show but how would we be certain of their positions and skirt them so that they wouldn't see us? And the five men on the bed? The five men? But there, sleep took mercy and I knew the place no more until the morning. When light came, I had the beginnings of tonsillitis.

CHAPTER 6

Training

The day started, like many another, with rain. We left Northern Ireland by the Larne to Stranraer cattle boat and caught the cattle train south, changing once at Birmingham. On arrival at Lavington, the three of us hung about for transport and eventually climbed into a three-ton truck, which deposited us, on a dank and misty afternoon, outside the orderly room at Tilshead. Having given our names, we then asked when tea was.

'Five o'clock,' came the answer, 'so you'd better get blancoing.'

'Blancoing?' we echoed.

'Yes, blancoing,' he snarled, 'Now, get out of my sight – I've got work to do.'

We stumbled through mud to our marquee and began to unload our kit. 'Do you suppose he meant what he said about blancoing?' I asked superfluously. He did. We blancoed every day for the next fourteen weeks.

Life was pretty dreadful in that place. There was absolutely no respite except on Sundays but even then one had to be careful and it was better to stay in bed. We did foot drill, arms drill, and backbreaking physical training and exercises without number and all the while, the RTUs (Returned to Units) were dropping out like flies. RSM Cowley was in his hey day then and sometimes he had so many in his guardroom under close arrest that he forgot why he had put them there and released them after parade. 'Smiler' Young took an instant dislike to me and I had to watch my Ps and Qs even more. 'Rolls-Royce voice and Ford Brainbox,' he shouted, 'that's what you are!' He was a Quartermaster Sergeant with an impressive array of Great War ribbons and I was but a lowly corporal. He put me on a charge once but I got off and so had to be even more careful. Then there was Foden, who always seemed to be coming around every corner but I managed to keep clear of him. The discipline was draconian but I managed to survive although, how, I do not know. Once, Captain Ogilvie put me on a charge for having my cross-straps laid out the wrong way on a kit inspection. 'You may think that I am being petty,' he explained, 'but the kind of man we want here, is a man who misses *nothing*! Seven days behind the guard!' I was relieved at not being returned to my unit and even more relieved when the list of names disappeared. For five lovely days we relaxed but on the last day, it reappeared at the last minute, so there was nothing for it but to go on parade. Standing behind the guard, with only one button polished and all my brasses unpolished, I awaited my fate. The tramping feet of Lieutenant Kershaw approached, paused and went on. Then they came up behind. There was another pause, a longer one this time. I had been caught and I knew it. My run of luck had come to an end and this time I would be definitely returned to my unit. 'A good turnout,' he remarked, 'and a good chinstrap too.' I swore a secret oath to smarten up again but almost lost the power of my legs with relief.

It was a waiting game. We waited for three weeks and then started all over again, to wait. We didn't know whether The Glider Pilot Regiment was due to start training or go back to its origins and be forgotten for ever, so we waited. We waited for news and we waited for no news and all the time we slogged away, at times being beaten nearly into the ground.

This might have gone on for ever but soon after Christmas we were sent down to Croughton to fly as 'Live Loads' on Hotspur gliders and we couldn't believe our luck. This meant acting as human guinea pigs for other pilots but we received assurances that no pilot would be allowed to fly us until his instructors were satisfied that he could and, on that basis, we accepted. (We did not have any option other than RTU. I recollect only one incident that went awry and it concerned a Lieutenant Cairns. We started off on a cross country for Stoke Orchard and all went well to start with. I was seated up against the bulkhead behind the main spar and so could not see much of what was going on. Cairns was flying first pilot, the flight seemed to be progressing well and we were nearing the end of our journey when suddenly and for no accountable reason, Cairns pulled off and we were in free flight. I didn't worry too much at the time because, I suppose, I couldn't see and didn't know the route anyway. Then we touched down and began to roll. On and on we went, at breakneck speed, or so it seemed, and now stones and bits of ploughed field came flying into our compartment through the floor. Suddenly, there was a bang, we rolled a few yards more and finally slithered to a stop. Shaken but unhurt, we stripped off the door and clambered out to find that we had left our wings behind in a hedge. Opposite us, and about fifty yards away, was one of the largest elm trees that I have ever seen. Cairns muttered an apology about the tug running out of fuel but how he came to that conclusion, I shall never know. Eventually a crash guard arrived in the shape of the United States Cavalry and we took off for home.

After Croughton, we moved on to Brize Norton where our duties were the same but in Airspeed Horsa gliders. By now 1943 was well advanced and as the days lengthened, we took more time off to stretch our limbs. I frequently visited Oxford and saw my mother and we used to play Bezique. She was in the ARP service then, as an ambulance driver, and I remember more than once having to hunt her all over Oxford to find out what spot she was in next. The Town Hall, the ARP Centre, her lodgings in one road or another, she had taken the decision to let our house to make ends meet. Her life seemed so remote then, so different to our Regiment's activities. At other times we went off to swim by the bridge near Filkins or drank beer and showed off in The Beehive or Coach and Horses. It was the customers of the former who were to witness a near fatality.

We used to have Whitleys as tugs then, mostly with inline engines and held together largely by the indefatigable work of the

RAF ground crews. Flown by pilots on rest and crewed by air navigators, gunners and wireless operators either on rest or under training, they worked relentlessly by day or night, pulling live or dead loads into the sky, round the circuit and down again for another trip. The 'Tail End Charlies' were usually trainee glider pilots and it was my turn, one night, to take my seat in the tail. The turret swung round, the rope was hitched up and away we went down the runway. Just another circuit, I thought, another landing, but then, as we turned across wind, the usual trail of sparks on the port side began to increase, soon to be followed by smoke. I compared it with the spark trail on the starboard side, and, yes, it was bigger. While I was looking from right to left and back again, the glider pulled off and we carried on alone. Suddenly, all smoke and sparks cleared to port and we were free of fire but vibrating badly. 'Nicky,' I called, 'there was a lot of smoke coming from the port engine but it has stopped now.' 'I know,' was the reply, 'I've put the fire out.' I realised then that something was wrong and we were flying asymmetrically on one engine. Then I heard Nicky's voice again. 'Hello Control – I haven't got enough height to make a decent approach, so I'm going round again.' There was nothing to do now but sit tight and hold on, for we were below parachute height. On the way round the circuit I could see the ground getting nearer and nearer and knew that we should never make it. Then came Nicky's voice a third time. 'The trouble is, we're going down instead of up.' It was true. Down and down we went but still, miraculously hitting nothing. It was when we passed a hangar below the height of its roof that I knew we shouldn't be able to go on for much longer. I tried desperately to remember what was ahead of us for I couldn't see out of the front. Then I began to pray. I don't know what words I used, but I prayed. I was still praying when we hit the ground and the port wing burst into flames, leaving a trail of fuel behind it. I lost no time in getting out, leaving my 'chute behind and ran round to the canopy. It was empty. Then I saw the others running for cover and followed.

I think, by now, most of the airfield seemed aware of what had happened, for all of them seemed to be closing in on the wreck.

We shouted uselessly and tried to warn them off and, as the tanks blew up, we shielded our eyes from the glare. At last, we got word through to them that there was no one alive in the machine. The crowd slowly and reluctantly dispersed, there having been only one casualty, a would-be rescuer with a small piece of metal in his stomach. The following morning, Nicky contracted chickenpox.

The summer saw us in Elementary Flying Training School (EFTS) at Booker, within spitting distance of High Wycombe and Marlow. We were split off into flights, and my flight found itself operating from Denham. My flying instructor was Flying Officer Brown and I have cause to remember only one other, Flying Officer Murphy. During the course of our training, Flying Officer Brown taught me much that I did not know but also taught me as a kind of equal, because of my alleged but totally untruthful account of flying hours on Tiger Moths. I had to admit that I knew nothing of the niceties of the Tiger Moth, only the rudiments of training. I think, on reflection, that Flying Officer Brown knew either nothing or everything about my aberration into falsehood but later experience has taught me to suspect the latter. However, teach me he did, and superbly. There was a rumour that he had been on flying boats, aircraft that required a very special kind of pilot, and was enjoying a six-month rest. He taught me to loop and he taught me to spin; he never quite taught me to roll but that was due not to his ability but to my sudden and hasty departure. He also taught me to take off and land without so much as mentioning one word of what it was about.

Only on one occasion was there any difference between us and I have to admit the fault lay squarely on my side. We had taken off to practise loops and climbed to about 6,000 feet. The first thing that you have to be aware of, he explained, was the danger or imminent danger of other aircraft in the air. This I took in. Then he added, in his usual mood of nonchalance and *savoir faire*, you had to pick a landmark; he picked one, a large, white house near Gerrards Cross. 'So that you know where you are when you come out of the manoeuvre,' he explained. Satisfied that all was well, he began the manoeuvre. 'Put your hands and feet on the controls,' he invited 'and follow me through as I do the loop.' The trim control went forward and then the stick. We were diving now, 100 knots, 120 knots. 'Now,' he said, 'up we go and over. Notice at the top of the loop, the engine cuts out, so we have to apply opposite rudder; then, as the engine picks up again, we gradually restore the balance on the rudder.' He restored the balance. I was breathless but determined. 'Now,' he continued, 'let's see what you can do.'

I looked round, up and down and I picked a landmark. OK,' I said, and pushed the stick and trim forward. Down we went and, at 120 knots, the nose came up. '*I've got her!*' exclaimed Brown suddenly, or at least, that's what I heard. 'OK,' I shouted down the Gosport tube, and relinquished all control. I think I assumed, at the time, that Brown knew what he was doing or had seen another aircraft; at any rate, I just sat and waited. Five thousand feet and still no response. Four thousand and still no call. Three thousand. At last came an angry voice on the Gosport. 'What, in the name of heaven, do you think you're doing?'

'Nothing sir,' I replied. 'You said that you had got her at the top of the loop, so I let go.'

'You bloody fool,' came the reply, 'I said *right rudder!*' It was the only time he had been known to swear.

The only other instructor that I remember was Flying Officer Murphy, as I have already recalled. He was among those Irishmen for whom everything goes wrong. He gathered us round a stationary Tiger Moth one day, to instruct us in the mysteries of starting the engine.

You first of all swing the prop four times with the engine off,' he explained, 'to suck in – like this.' He suited action to his words. 'Next, you swing it with the engine on – Contact.'

'Contact,' came the answer from the cockpit and Murphy swung. He swung it for four or five times but nothing happened, so he swung it again. A small twig, sticking up out of the ground about four inches high was bothering him, so he bent down to pluck it up. It resisted, so he pulled it again. It still resisted, so he

Godfrey Freeman.

A Handley Page Halifax takes to the air towing a Horsa glider.

The Airspeed Horsa was Britain's first troop-transport glider. 3,655 were built and each could carry 25 fully equipped soldiers.

The Horsa was of an all wood construction and was flown with a two-man crew. The Y shaped towing line can clearly be seen in this take-off shot.

A Horsa landing at its base airfield. On operations when being towed during a long distance flight and landing on rough terrain the two main landing wheels of its tricycle undercarriage would be jettisoned to reduce drag. The nose wheel and a shock absorbing runner under the belly reduced the landing impact.

Lieutenant Henry Cole.

Glider Pilot Regiment 19 Flight B Squadron on 18 July 1944. Godfrey Freeman is 4th from the right top row.

The immediate escape area.

The escape window.

The Paleis at Het Loo.
The hospital prison!

A return to the landing zone.

Pat Mahoney (left) and the author.

Willem (far right) and Hennie Zegers (2nd left) family home. An escape route stop-over.

stamped it down and returned to the swinging. He waited patiently while he swung and swung. Eventually, he gave up. 'There comes a time when a man has to acknowledge defeat.' He muttered gloomily and opened the small compartment behind the pilot's seat whence he emerged with a sizeable pipe wrench. Opening the cowling, he smote the impulse starter a hefty blow and tried again. Still no response. He tried the twig again; again, no response. 'I guess,' he announced heavily, 'we'll have to try another day.' We parted ranks to let him through as he shambled back to the flight office.

Once, with a pupil named Charlie Pinner, he displayed complete unconcern in the face of possible disaster. By coincidence it was also during a practice on loops. Pinner had taken control and was already diving; as the needle on the Air Speed Indicator passed the 125 mark, Murphy was heard to ask whether Pinner was married. On receiving a negative reply, he then wondered whether Pinner had a girlfriend. Pinner replied that he had not, so Murphy enquired after his parents. By this time, the needle was nearing 140 and, on hearing that the parents were alive and well, Murphy delivered himself of an opinion. 'If you ever want to see them again,' he suggested, 'I think you had better pull out of this dive right now!'

But time's winged chariot was at our backs and our EFTS was cut short. Unlike other intakes, we were sent on to Glider Training School at Stoke Orchard without any night flying instruction and then, after a few weeks, back to Brize Norton. At Brize Norton, we now began to fly the aircraft that would carry us into battle. Huge by comparison with anything that we had flown before, the Horsa Mk 1 could carry twenty-five fully armed infantrymen; it could also carry a jeep and six-pounder gun with gun crew, or a jeep, trailer, motorcycle and five other ranks or almost any other load that the mind of man could devise. Bangalore torpedoes, parts of Bailey bridges, fuel, ammunition, all the paraphernalia of war except tanks and heavy guns could be transported to and unloaded right on target. Its elder brother, the super heavy Hamilcar, which we did not fly, carried tanks or seventeen-pounders with their Morris Portees. By day and night, we had to learn to fly these aircraft and land them, first on the runway and then, little by little, on a more closely defined area. They had enormous flaps like barn doors that came down to eighty degrees, and the trick was to stand on your nose and come down in a nearly vertical dive, pulling out at the last moment and settling on the ground like a giant bat. This particular manoeuvre was known as the 'Slash' and in addition, we practised a low release and dive approach. This latter, however, was discontinued after a number of gliders failed to make the field.

We continued training in this way until we were sent to Holmsley South, an airfield without a serviceable runway, so we had to do our flying from Hurn. Here for a while we shared our camp with some United States troops and there were a few WAAFs on the station. The going was fairly easy except for run-marches. These were a refined form of torture that everyone came to fear and dread. You put on full battle-order and steel helmet, picked up your rifle and fell in by flights. 'Double March!' would come the order and away you would go, not at the usual double pace but a larger, more stretching stride. About three miles up the road you broke into a quick time for a few hundred yards and then started again. This might continue for anything up to fifteen miles without any halts or stops until the last two hundred yards or so and then 'Last man goes on guard tonight!' came the shout and you pelted in any old how, anxious not to be the last man in. As far as I know, no one ever was but there was no sense in chancing one's arm. It was also a wonderful cure for a hangover!

Flying from Hurn by night was a weird experience but a peaceful one. Sometimes I flew with pilots who had little or no experience of night flying but managed to control the haunting feeling that we might not land as we should. Nevertheless I was always glad to be down again and in one piece. The night was a blackout of everything but the tug's tail light in front and a dim outline of wings and a tail. The flare path beneath gradually receded and then we were left, joined together by three hundred feet of rope and floating in absolute darkness. Now and then there were stars and, occasionally, the moon but for the most part I remember flying in almost total blackness.

On one of these occasions six gliders took off on an exercise and disappeared for an hour on a cross-country, one of them flown by a staunch Irish Catholic named Danny. During this interval, however, the wind changed through a full 180 degrees, so the airfield was changed round to suit the wind. Flying continued, once more, as normal. No one gave the matter any further thought until the six gliders returned, when it became plain, too late, that the pilots were unaware of the wind change and were coming in to land on the original flare path, but with the wind dangerously behind them. (Birds and aircraft alike always land heading into the wind for a safe and controlled landing, so as to obtain maximum flying airspeed over their wings, with minimum flying speed over the ground.) A flare path looks much the same whichever end that you view it from, except for a few markers, and down they came, helter-skelter, all six of them landing downwind.

Miraculously, they missed the towpath and tore on out of sight into the night, whence a series of bumps, bangs and crunches announced that they had reached their final destinations. A rapid round-up assured all present that no one was seriously hurt but Danny had distinguished himself. His nose had penetrated a Methodist chapel and on the wall opposite him hung a large sign with the words 'Trust in the Lord and ye shall be saved'. 'I trust,' remarked Danny, 'that nobody thinks that I am religiously biased in any way.'

On another occasion a night flying sergeant found himself being towed through cloud. He hung on as long as he could, hoping that he would soon emerge into clear air again but luck was not with him that night and he eventually had to pull off. Circling round looking for a forced landing site, he soon cleared cloud base and was both amazed and delighted to see a flare path about a thousand feet below him. With no more ado, he went into the circuit pattern and started an approach but, as he made his final turn in to land, he noticed that the flare path was undulating. Dismissing the phenomenon as some trick of the light, or lack of it, on Perspex, he pressed on and a few seconds later made a perfect landing on the Sunderland flying boat flare path in Poole Harbour! There was at that time, a much-used slogan 'Remember Pearl Harbor', to commemorate the Japanese attack and to urge the American forces on to greater zeal. The following night, the Sergeant returned to his hut to find a hastily illuminated scroll decorating the wall above his bedside: 'Remember Poole Harbour' it read.

Autumn gave way to winter and winter to spring. One day a Major Croot called us all together and gave us a pep talk. I don't remember how it started but I recollect very well how it ended. 'You'll be going on leave,' he declared, 'and after that you'll be going to your battle stations. So, if you're going to get married, get married, and if you're going to get divorced, get divorced, because....' Then he paused to give effect to his words, 'There will be gaps in our ranks before your next leave. Mark my words, there will be gaps.' Croot survived Arnhem but later became one of the 'gaps'. A Dakota carrying him and some others to Palestine, hit the Pyrenees in a snowstorm and he was among those who did not return. This I learnt from Staff Sergeant Ainsworth, MM, who himself lost all his toes, through frostbite, on the same mission but that, as they say, is another story.

We left Hurn by air and it fell to our lot to carry kit bags. I don't know how many of these there were but you couldn't see down the fuselage past the front door and the undercarriage landing 'skid' was touching the ground. I pointed this out to Lieutenant Henry Cole, my first pilot, but he seemed unmoved. 'I expect it'll be all right,' he muttered, giving the statutory pull on the tail. The way to test a Horsa for correct loading was to pull down on the tail. If the nose didn't come up, or come up too easily, there was a misloading; if it came up and went down again more or less evenly, all was well. This time it came up and went down but all the way back to Brize Norton I flew with my heart in my mouth and was seldom so relieved to be on the ground again! I think one of the reasons for my fears at the time, was that we no longer carried parachutes. These had been issued to us by the RAF for every flight from EFTS onwards but were withdrawn when we were posted to an operational squadron. Now we had to fly with a Rexine cushion instead and the difference made me, at any rate, more conscious of what could go wrong and more anxious that nothing should be amiss before take-off. On one dreadful occasion, while on a cross-country flight, the tail section of a Horsa had parted company with the main body at a height of about two thousand feet; twenty-five soldiers and both pilots had gone hurtling to their doom and, though I tried not to think of such things, they had a knack of coming back to me. Once, we picked up from Netheravon a new type of Horsa with four quick-release bolts holding the tail section in place. We took off and all seemed to be going well until, as we were approaching Salisbury Cathedral spire, there came a resounding 'crack' from the rear of the glider. I looked at Henry, who returned my glare, but neither of us spoke! A little while later, there came a second 'crack'. I contained myself as long as I could and then volunteered, 'Do you think it would be a good idea if I went back down the fuselage to see what is making that noise?' Henry appeared to consider. 'Yes, I think so,' he said at last, 'yes I should go and take a look.' I went back down and checked. One-two-three-four; all the release bolts seemed to be in order. Then I noticed the door. It had not been properly fastened on take-off and had sprung partly open; first one catch giving way and then the other. I made the door fast and returned to my seat. 'It's all right,' I said as nonchalantly as I could, 'it was only the door, I fixed it.'

We flew by day and we flew by night and we carried out our mass landings, of twenty, fifty and even a hundred gliders at a time. Gradually, I came to know Henry Cole better. He was older than I, but somewhat shorter in height, with dark, almost saturnine, good looks, which belied his true self. Due to an unfortunate habit of keeping his pipe in his field dressing pocket, it invariably broke, so he mended it with rubber tubing. As he walked, so his pipe would bounce up and down in time with his pace; this coupled with a three quarter length gunner's coat, lent him a faintly swashbuckling air and set him slightly apart from the rest. He said little but saw much and eventually took to wearing a yellow scarf, decorated with foxes' heads, to fly in. By and by we became quite close friends but he was an officer and I was a sergeant, so there the relationship halted so to speak. I never knew anything of his family, friends or fears. Once we flew a massed landing, ending up before the royal family at Netheravon, when we put down about a hundred gliders in five minutes. On another occasion, we flew General Urquart. As we waited to board our Horsa, the General paused to exchange banter with his *aides-de-camp*. 'Do you suppose,' he asked, 'that these sick bags are good for morale?' He was referring to the brown paper bags provided for those whose stomachs could not accept the battering of a bumpy ride on a gusty day. 'I should think sir,' one replied, 'that they're good for morale if they are close to you.' The remark was received with polite laughter and we climbed aboard. An hour and a half's flying time found us passing over Guildford and heading out for open country. The General's head appeared in the cockpit. 'Can you tell me where we are?' he asked. I told him as best as I could but we were over fields at the time so it was impossible to give an exact pinpoint. The next time I looked around, his head was buried deep into the brown paper bag.

Apart from these two incidents, however, our training passed uneventfully enough except when Henry misjudged an approach on landing and we lost a nose wheel coming in through a hedge. The leg came up through the floorboards and injured one of our 'live load' but not seriously thank heaven. The jolt gave both of us a timely warning to exercise even more care in the future.

CHAPTER 7

The First Attempt

The tonsillitis grew worse as the day wore on and I dallied with the idea of using it as an excuse to 'duck out' of the escape. What better reason could I give, other than a broken arm or leg? It would relieve me of the necessity of risking life and limb, exonerate me completely and I should be left behind with regrets. 'Poor old Freeman,' they might say. 'What a pity, what bad luck, just when he was about to escape, he had to go and get tonsillitis.' The more I thought of it, the better it seemed and eventually I went and saw Major Coke, only I did not say directly what was in my mind; instead, I asked him what he thought. 'You must make up your own mind whether you are coming or not,' he said. 'Let me know later how you feel.' From that moment on, I was in an agony of indecision. On the one hand was peace, tranquillity, release from the nagging fears that made the night so hideous; on the other hand, as then I thought, honour, glory and renown. Indeed, what further proof would be needed that I was a Man? I prowled around finding things to do, looking at my watch, scratching my name and number on blank identity tags that Pat had provided from somewhere, rewinding bandages, anything to take my mind off the decision that I had to eventually make. The day wore into afternoon, the afternoon into evening. Eventually, I could stand it no longer. As though in a daze, I sought out Major Coke again. 'Well?' he asked. I opened my mouth to speak and heard my voice coming from a long way away. 'I think I'll be all right sir,' I said, 'I mean, I think I'll make it.'

As the night came on we lay on our beds biding our time. Fully dressed but under cover of our blankets, we waited for the last calls to be made by the orderlies, for the lights to go out and, for those able to, to settle into a reasonably untroubled sleep. Then the preparations began. First of all we had to don our boots, which we had kept carefully hidden for days under our beds. Next we armed ourselves with a toggle-rope each from the curtain restrainers and picked up our Red Cross rations. Lastly, the hose pipe had to be collected from the open hallway. This was a critical undertaking, for the guard was placed the other side of the door, but it was achieved in silence and we made our way to the window, which was to provide the exit for our escape. The hose was gradually paid out of the window and one end made fast to a bed on which five men were lying. Out went Pat Mahoney. The Major was to follow and I was to be last out. We were to wait until Pat had reached the bottom where he was to hold the hose away from the window. Suddenly Pat was back at the window and we were hauling him in. There was no time for explanations; we flew back to bed and buried ourselves under the blankets. What had gone wrong? What had happened? For an hour we waited but there was no reaction from the Germans, so we came out again to consult Pat Mahoney.

It seemed that when Pat thought he had got down to the bottom, he had in fact got down as far as the ledge of the window directly below and, turning, he had banged his elbow on a glass pane. There was a party on at the time and he could not be sure but someone, a woman he thought, had rushed across the room as though frightened by the noise. Needless to say, he had taken the decision to turn back and come up the hose as fast as he could. I must say that, in spite of everything, I could not help but admire the speed with which he had returned; he must have climbed up faster than a monkey! The question remained, what were we to do now? After a lot of humming and hawing, we decided to postpone for another twenty-four hours and then try again. On that, we broke up reluctantly and went back to bed.

Shortly before lights-out, Arni appeared at my bedside. 'Sergeant Freeman,' he said, 'I do not think I have your boots.'

Had he tried, he could not have timed things better. 'My boots?' I replied, turning over all the possibilities in my mind and finding none that would answer, 'Oh my boots… Of course!' Reluctantly, but with as great a show of readiness as I could muster, I groped around and found the offending footwear. 'Here we are,' I said, smiling. 'Thank you,' replied Arni, 'and good night.' 'Good night,' I replied, cursing inwardly and turned over as though to sleep until morning. A decent interval after he had left, I got out of bed to see what could be done. Finally, I cut out two foot liners from the lino under my bed. Inside my socks they would provide protection for my feet for a while, at any rate.

CHAPTER 8

Missing D-Day

D-Day had come and gone but with it, remarkably few casualties and some distinctions. I had not taken part and nor had my flight. Such was the success of the D-Day landings, put by some at ninety-eight per cent, that our reserve flight was not needed. We had missed the big one, we thought, but there would be others. We were right, there were; three or four if I remember. Each time, we were fully loaded and ready to go and then an order would come through that we had been stood down. On one or two occasions, we unloaded gliders and then loaded them again. It was a farce but a dangerous farce. It drained away resolve and replaced it with indifference. We never knew whether it was real or not and it set our nerves on edge. We reacted in a variety of ways; I myself took to drinking and drank on a Homeric scale until my funds ran dry, then I would wait until the next payday and start again. This might have gone on for some time but then along came Arnhem. It was just another name in a growing list. Was it the fourth or fifth? I cannot remember. Did it matter? No. It would be cancelled, just like all the others had been. We loaded gliders and then unloaded them again. This time we flew down to Manston in Kent. We hung about for two or three days, alerted and then stood down. It was a waiting game again. The more adventurous spirits among us went into Margate or Ramsgate and cashed the contents of our escape packs. Then, one morning, we woke up and word went round that this time was for real.

We couldn't believe it. Even when the Albermarle that was to be our 'tug' swung into line ahead and took up the slack of the tow rope, we still only half believed it. Gradually the rope tightened and we started to roll down the runway. There was a bump or two or three and then we were airborne. Seconds later, our tug was airborne too. Slowly we climbed to about 2,500 feet and headed for Canterbury to join the others. In the glider were Major Jones, Sergeant Doughty, three other ranks, a Jeep, a trailer and a motorcycle, comprising the headquarters of the First Airlanding Anti-Tank.

From all over southern Britain, it seemed, aircraft were converging into an endless stream, which sailed on and on over roads, railways, rivers, over built-up areas and farmland, until at last it crossed the coastline and we were out over the North Sea. Halifaxes, Stirlings, Dakotas and our Albermarles, each with a glider on tow, swept on in an relentless throng, while above, below and on the same level, fighter aircraft kept station to guard us from attack. On our way out, we met Bomber Command coming back. Their work was done; ours was beginning. We flew on, terribly slowly it seemed, while the shores of Britain receded behind us. Down below, we could see ships, floating like models on a sea of glass. Whatever else we were going to meet that day, at least the weather was smiling. There was a strange comfort sitting there with Henry Cole, as though we were on exercise. I had to remind myself that this was the real thing. We could just make out the Dutch coastline now and, as it drew nearer, some lights began to flash as though the sun were catching a distant window-pane. I pointed this out to Henry and asked him what he made of it. Before he could answer, four Mustang fighter aircraft floated down out of nowhere and made hell for leather for the flashes. Now we were over land and a few puffs of flak appeared, bursting some two hundred yards or more to starboard but I didn't see anyone hit. There was something exorable about the stream and its forging on, as though nothing could or would stop it. Below now were fields and floods, a glider down in one of them and a windmill sitting completely surrounded by water. Not long to go now. I looked at Henry but he was concentrating on keeping station behind the tug. I looked around and about and could see nothing but our Horsa gliders, with the occasional, larger, Hamilcar tank-carrying glider, all heading one way with one aim in view. It was an awesome sight and I began to feel part of a machine, hauled along 'willy nilly' to take part in... but here my imagination failed me. It was my first operation and I did not know what to expect.

'Right, here we go,' said Henry and pushed down the big tow-rope release lever. We slowed down to a gliding speed as our tug sped away ahead of us and began to lose height. Nearer and nearer came the ground and I waited for the first shots. None came. Half flap came down, then full flap and we were 'standing on our nose'. We then flattened out, there was a familiar bump and jolt and now we were rolling. A few more yards and we stopped. We were down in one piece and had landed unopposed.

The first job was to get the tail section off and to get the load out of the glider. We did this with some difficulty and then went over to an overturned Hamilcar to see what could be done to help. He had come in at too fast a run, his wheels had dug into the soft soil of the potato patch, which was our landing zone, and over he had gone, gun, Morris Portee and all. We managed to extricate the first pilot but the second pilot was dead, the seat back having broken his neck. Then we turned our attention to the members of the gun crew. All around us, paratroopers were dropping, picking up their gear and making their way to their rendezvous. We got one man out, then another but there we had to stop. There were two legs sticking out from the side of the glider and they kept kicking. I tried to ignore them for I knew that nothing could be done. Short of a crane and hoist, there was no way of righting the glider. We had to leave him and gradually, the kicking stopped and became still. It was a bad moment. We went back to our load, climbed aboard one of the Jeeps and set off for the woods.

There was some hanging about here while we deliberated what to do; there seemed no real spirit of urgency. Major Jones had a quick 'snack and snort' from his hip flask and we listened to the six o'clock news bulletin from England. I could only guess that we were waiting until nearer the fall of darkness before we broke cover from the woods. Finally we set off, still unopposed, for the bridge at Arnhem. Some sporadic bursts of fire started to break out here and there together with a form of rocket that made a noise like ripping canvas, flew overhead from time to time but landed miles the other end of the landing zone. It was still light and soon we passed one of the first enemy casualties, General Cussins. Further on up the road, we met a husband and wife who were out on bicycles, to see the 'fun' I suppose. The husband asked for an English cigarette, so I gave him one of the three which were left in my ration pack. In exchange, we were offered a drink of apricot brandy. Soon we caught up with the mainstream who were pushing on for Arnhem Bridge. They were a motley crew. There were men pushing handcarts, an old Mercedes sports car in the middle of the column, which had been pressed into service, troops riding, some walking but all pressing on for Arnhem. From time to time we halted and then pushed on again. Still, no opposition; it began to grow dark eventually and the stops became more frequent. Gradually, we approached the bridge, occasionally asking where the Germans were, only to be told that they had left. We pulled up by the riverside and while we were waiting, a burst of small arms fire came from our left. Then there was silence. Suddenly, around seven o'clock, all hell broke loose up at the front.

It seemed as though both sides were letting loose with everything that they had got. We couldn't see far enough ahead to make out what was going on and could only lie and wait. On my left, some troops were digging a mortar pit and up ahead, from time to time, came a German MG42 in bursts, firing from right to left, his tracers laying a lethal path across what could be seen of the street. The dead must be piling up on both sides, I thought, as the cannonade continued unabated. There were mortar bombs, grenades and small arms fire and I could not see how they could continue for much longer. We learnt later that an ammunition dump had been hit by a flame-thrower but, not knowing at the time, wasted nearly a whole hour waiting for a lull in the supposed battle. Finally, we moved into a building, which turned out to be the municipal waterworks office but for that night it was welcome shelter. Henry and I moved into the cellars, collected files together to make a rough bed and soon fell asleep. It was the last sleep but one that I was to know for three days.

It is difficult to recall events as they occurred; all seemed part of a vast kaleidoscope of events that merged into one but remained essentially different. There was the prisoner, an old man judging by his appearance, nearing sixty, whose greatest fear was that we should shoot him out of hand. He went into the bag without much trouble. Then there was the Dutch interpreter, one minute with us, then gone the next, 'whoof', just like that. I have recollections of some twenty-odd prisoners, sitting with their little fibre suitcases, only too glad to surrender and give us no further trouble. I was put in charge of them for a while. Then someone needed cigarettes and I climbed up to hand over a packet of 'Typ 2½' to a signaller on a higher part of the building. Then there was the German officer, who seemed strangely out of context with his surroundings, that I was put to guard for a while. I sat opposite him for an hour or two while we exchanged pleasantries. He had, it seemed, been losing vehicles one by one all the way from Paris, from whence he had started with ninety-six and had now lost everything in Arnhem. He showed me pictures of his wife and children back home while I sat, my Tommy-gun pointed unwaveringly at his breast, ready for the slightest move to escape on his part. There was the house where I had found the English version of the *Book of Common Prayer*, looked up the twenty-first psalm and read it while a six-pounder blasted away at the bridge, bringing down more plaster from the ceiling with every round that it fired. There was a meeting with another glider pilot. He was covered all over from head to foot in white dust and he and I exchanged a brief greeting. I asked about a girlfriend that we had both been chasing but received a curt response in reply.

All this time, firing was, more or less, continuous. During the lulls, we climbed over walls into the next house up the street and then the next and so on. We did this three or four times and then started coming back. Somewhere along the line I had lost Henry and never saw him again. It was chaotic but being in action for the first time, I imagined that it was always like this. In a side road was an abandoned German truck and, during another lull, I ran round the corner to see if there was any food in it. The driver's rifle was still beside the seat and, with the aid of this, I broke open the tool locker. Inside were a couple of bottles, a tin of sardines and some cheese. I pocketed the latter, placed one bottle on the window sill and ran back into the house with the other. The first bottle had gone when I got back but I still had the second and took it upstairs to make some sort of meal. There didn't seem to be much going on at the time, so after eating the sardines and drinking some of the wine, I decided to catch up on some sleep on a large double bed. I don't know how long the sleep lasted but the next thing I remember was being shaken violently awake by a paratrooper. 'Come on,' he shouted, 'we're getting out of here!' I stumbled after him down the stairs, out of the back door and over the wall into the next house. Nobody seemed to know what was going on. We went upstairs to the next floor and looked cautiously out of the window. There was no one about except a man in a dark brown suit standing in a doorway opposite. He was wearing a white helmet and appeared to be interested in something further down the street towards the bridge. We debated shooting him but decided to let him off as he might be a Dutchman. At the back of the house was a small landing and some paratroopers were showing an interest in a church tower about two hundred yards distant. There was a balustrade round the top where the spire met the tower, built of stone uprights with a coping along the top. One corner of this balustrade was a bit darker than the rest and could be concealing an enemy. There was only one way to find out. I broke some panes of glass away, poked my Tommy-gun through, took careful aim and fired a short burst. I don't know to this day what was there but there was more smoke than could have come from five rounds of ammunition. Then it was downstairs and over the wall into the next house again.

By and by we worked our way back to the waterworks building and by this time it was growing dark. A Lieutenant in the Corps of Military Police was looking for someone, anyone, to accompany him on a search patrol. It wasn't abundantly clear what we were searching for but reluctantly I complied. I broke some panes away with the Tommy-gun again and we passed through a window. Outside it was now dark and we could barely see each other. The officer went first and I followed. After all, it was his show. He would make one advance and then I would follow. We made about two jumps this way and then I froze. Straight ahead of me was a German infantryman, hatless but unmistakeable, in the lying load position with his rifle out in front of him. Inch by inch, I moved forward again, wary of any movement that he might make. He made none, so I eased forward again. He was lying a little to my left. Slowly, my heart making strange noises in my chest, I moved closer. Then the truth became clear; he was dead. I didn't feel like any more that night and neither did the MP. He came back soon after and we both returned to the safety of the waterworks building. The last thing that I remember doing that night was dishing out cigarettes to the old Dutchman who was sheltering in the cellars. He took them gratefully, about six of them, and proceeded to break away the paper, retaining the tobacco in the palm of his hand. I expected him to produce a pipe and fill it but he thrust the tobacco into his mouth and, with a wink and a nod, began to chew. Then the bombardment began again. I think it continued for hours and, in the lulls, we put the fires out. After the fifth or sixth time, there was no water or sand or anything that would help now. Colonel Frost, reluctant to the last, finally ordered the white sheet to be hung out. The British garrison, with orders to hold the bridge for a maximum of forty-eight hours, had held it twice as long but, at last, it proved too much for them. Wearily, we slung down our arms and awaited the enemy.

CHAPTER 9

The Escape

I was to go down the hosepipe last, as planned. It was a Sunday night and all was quiet inside the building. We had timed the guard to a nicety and outside a wind was blowing and a rain was driving as though it would squall all night but by the time I got to the hosepipe it was wet and slippery. I covered the first few feet alright and then began to slither. Gradually I lost control and landed, as I thought, on one of those iron rings that are put across the corners of lawns to prevent people walking them down. There was a stifled curse from Pat Mahoney at the time but I took no notice of it. Exactly thirty-six years later I discovered the true cause of his anger but, for the moment, all we could do now was to run for cover. We made the trees and then the wall. I can't remember now whether we climbed over but the next thing was that we were in the house of one of the royal servants. Standing there in his nightshirt he gave directions to the Major, while his wife looked on apprehensively. After a brief description of the way out of the town, he opened the door again and let us out. With the wind still blowing and the rain still splattering on the leaves, we made our way down a path that we had never seen until we came in sight of a sentry box. We still kept the same order, with the Major in the lead, Pat following and myself last. At this point, I got cut off temporarily until Pat came back to fetch me. 'Whatever on earth are you doing?' he demanded angrily but before I could make my reply, he vanished into the wind and darkness again and I followed. We made our way out of the area and into the town.

The streets were deserted when we came to them and there was an eerie silence. We plodded on after the Major, who seemed to know the way. Evidently, the weather was keeping most German guards inside. We dodged from one front garden to another, taking cover and then moving on. I was tempted to think of the days in the Oxford side roads, when all was at risk for a bar of chocolate. After some time we were clear of the town and came to a large country house standing on its own. We banged on the door repeatedly but received no reply. We tried the victory 'V' signal, three shorts and a long, but still no reply. Either the Major had muddled his directions or the twenty-four-hour delay had been enough to send the Underground to cover. Whatever the reason, there was only one thing to do now, press on, so we did.

Pretty soon we came to a wood. We were not too sure of our directions now but with the aid of an escape compass, approximately the size of a sixpence, we kept going roughly north-west. My improvised footwear had gradually worn out over the last mile or two, so that I was now forced to continue in bare feet. At first I put them down gingerly, expecting sharp pebbles or thorns to puncture my soles any minute but, little by little, I got used to it and put them down more and more firmly until I was walking normally. From time to time we stopped and cocked our ears to make sure that no one was following us; the rain was making a noise on the leaves exactly like footsteps. It was still pitch dark when eventually we came to a road and paused for a moment to take stock. The Major inquired after my feet and I told him that I was quite prepared to press on but found the going easier across country as distinct from roads. Nevertheless, we followed the road for a bit until the first truck came our way. Fortune favoured us again, the enemy had dug slit trenches alongside the road as a precaution against air attack and into one of these we piled as the truck rolled on towards Apeldoorn. Soon we were out again and moving on when there was another truck and another dive into the slit trench. We carried on in this way until we came to an abrupt halt. Up ahead, a German was shouting but we could not catch his words. Then another sound;

a rumble, a creak, a clank and a drone….tanks! We couldn't see them in the dark but from the sound of it, there were quite a few and they were lagering up for the night. Pat was all for going forward to see what was happening but was restrained by the Major. We turned off the other side of the road into the woods again and made off once more, soon leaving the sound of the *Panzers* far behind.

We struggled on, always with a hindward glance, now and again halting for breath and to consult the compass. At length we came to a section of wood divided by fire paths – paths through which anyone attempting to extinguish a fire might pass, or where a fire might be extinguished before proceeding further. It was still dark but we decided to progress along the fire paths, tuning off to the right when the occasion presented itself and then continuing. It was a wearisome business but the distance between us and, any possible pursuers, grew ever less and all the time we managed to maintain a north-westerly direction. Our greatest fear was of tracker dogs but, happily, we encountered none. Once or twice, I fancied I could hear barking in the distance and we stopped to listen but then pushed on. We kept up the pace until dawn broke and found us on the outskirts of the wood.

CHAPTER 10

The Dutch Underground

After some deliberation, the Major decided to go ahead and reconnoitre. Pat and I took up positions where one fire path crossed another and together we awaited the return of the Major while keeping an eye open for any unwelcome intrusion from the east. No such intrusion occurred and, eventually, the Major returned. He signalled us to follow and we did, breaking cover and discerning at the edge of the wood a little farmhouse. He beckoned us on and we followed hesitantly, with a glance to left and right, for wariness had now become a habit. At last we found ourselves within the doors of the farmhouse and stood waiting while the farmer kept up a running conversation with the Major, all the time eyeing us suspiciously.

It seemed that the farmer could not make up his mind whether we were really British or whether it was a clever ruse of the *Gestapo* to ascertain his loyalties. The Major could speak only German and this led to his suspicion. Pat and I could speak no Dutch and precious little German. After what seemed a long while, he relented and decided that we were British. Thereafter, there was nothing that was too much trouble for him to do but first he bade us, by signs and gestures, to go back to the woods whence we had come and wait while he made various enquiries. A short while afterwards he reappeared with quantities of straw and indicated that we should make ourselves as comfortable as possible while we waited.

I don't know how it came about but I think it was by drawing lots. At any rate, I had the first spell off duty, while the other two went to keep watch at the end of the fire path. Gratefully, I covered myself with straw and, soon forgetting all cares but the immediate one of lack of sleep, fell into a deep and long-awaited slumber. It wasn't long before they were back, shaking me violently by the shoulder. 'For God's sake,' they remonstrated, 'make less noise, can't you?' I struggled to understand. 'What?' I replied. 'Noise? What noise?' It seemed that I had begun to snore, loudly enough to be heard some fifty yards away. I apologised and muttered something about turning over and sleeping on my side or stomach to avoid a repetition and did so. A short while later, they were back and shaking me again. It hadn't worked and they were genuinely concerned. Reluctantly I struggled to my feet, apologised and agreed to stand watch instead. I think it was at that moment that the farmer reappeared once more and ushered us back to the house.

Once inside again and relieved of the necessity to identify ourselves, I had a chance to take stock of our new surroundings. The room was small and appeared to be the only one in the house, except for the bedroom, which was directly above it. For furnishing, it only had a few upright chairs, four or five, and a table. The floor was of plain wood and, I think, boasted a square of carpet. On one side stood the kitchen range, with such pots and pans as could be mustered, while opposite was the window and at either end were cupboards which, on being opened, proved to be sleeping bunks for the two children of the household or others who might happen by. Next to the window was the front door, which opened onto a garden that provided, amongst other things, tobacco. Opposite this door was another that opened directly into the stable where a cow and pig were housed. Also in the stable, was a huge collection of junk, ranging from farm implements to disused pots and pans, from which the farmer eventually produced a pair of shoes to cover my feet. I did not know the farmer's name then and did not ask it, for if pressed, one could not reveal secrets one did not know. Apart from these rooms, there was the hayloft above the bedroom and that was all. There was certainly no bathroom and I doubt there was a toilet but cannot now remember. Within this small haven lived the farmer, his wife, two children and a girl from Arnhem who had been driven out by the fighting there.

The first night, Pat, the Major and I spent on the floor. From time to time, I awoke and could hear the cow humming next door. It was a restful sound, seeming to betoken peace and urging one to relax. The children slept in their cupboards and the girl from Arnhem upstairs with the farmer's wife. It was a far cry from Apeldoorn and I began to wonder what had become of the rest of them there. What had been the reaction to our leaving? Had they got the hosepipe up again and stacked it away neatly before they were caught? Dr Schamer and Arni – how had they taken the news, which, by now, must have come to their ears? Would there be repercussions, punishments more severe than the last one? Well, at any rate, there wasn't much they could do to them except dock their cigarettes and tobacco, tighten the guards or, perhaps, patrol the area more frequently. I nodded off. This time, nothing and nobody woke me and I slept fast through until morning.

Somewhere in the early hours of the next day, when the light was beginning to steal through the window, the farmer appeared and started to clear out the fire. We dozed on for a while until his wife came down to wake the children for breakfast and school and then stirred our limbs to make way for them. The girl from Arnhem was evidently having a lie-in. After breakfast, there was a brief moment of farewells before the two children left the house, slipping off their house shoes and stepping into their clogs as they went. The whole household did this, so that no mud was brought into the house from outside, so it remained remarkably clean. Occasionally a little straw had to be swept back into the stable area but apart from that, no dirt was allowed to intrude. There were, however, an unbelievable number of flies. These, Pat and I made sport with, catching them by hand on the window panes but, for all my attempts, I could not match Pat's prowess. However, there was little else to do except wait or roll cigarettes or just chat.

About this time a conversation took place, which I did not

relish but had to listen to. It concerned discipline in the RAF and the Major was vehement in his disposal of it. The RAF, according to him, were an ill-disciplined bunch with no pride in their appearance and precious little, if any, in anything else.

I don't know what had got into the man but before I could speak, Pat Mahoney was hard at it in defence of the RAF. 'If you had seen those Dakotas coming in to drop our supplies, you wouldn't say that; how can you say that in view of what they did?' The Major hummed and hawed for a bit. 'Well, I must say I didn't see any of it then.' Both men had been down the road in Oosterbeek, so I had to take a back seat. 'The discipline of the RAF was never in question,' asserted Pat Mahoney. 'No, I suppose not,' agreed the Major. Pat and I went on catching flies.

By and by, lunchtime came around. I forget now what lunch consisted of but remember that whatever it was, it was welcome; anything would have been at that time. Then I think we had a little more sleep. Time wore on. Eventually, the children came back from school, were fed and then went to bed while we stayed up a little longer. The farmer showed us how to cut tobacco, first in coarse strips for a pipe and then in fine strips for cigarettes. He let us try, laughingly putting us right when we tried and failed and then succeeded. After a while he sought about and produced a pipe, which had been little smoked and he wished me to have. I kept it throughout the escape but then, to my chagrin, lost it. It was a Meerschaum pipe and had a picture, which became more plain as each fill of the bowl was smoked. Pat Mahoney stuck to his cigarettes; the Major, so far as I remember, smoked little or nothing.

We spent another night on the wooden floor, not knowing what was to become of us but sleeping soundly none the less. As I went to sleep, dreams of Apeldoorn receded but new ones took their place. What if the Germans caught us? Would we be sent back to Apeldoorn to answer for our sins or would we be shipped straight back to Germany with a belligerent guard and no hope of escape? Would we be shot, perhaps running for safety, while the farmer and his wife looked on, powerless, themselves only minutes from the firing squad? The speculations were numerous and always pessimistic. Eventually, I fell asleep again.

Dawn broke as usual and with it, no sign of rain. The farmer came down and tended to the fire, his wife followed later and the children went off to school as usual. The girl from Arnhem put in an appearance, evidently refreshed, but we couldn't communicate with her all that well, except to reassure her of our *bona fides* and to wish her well. While we were trying to establish further communications, the farmer returned in a hurry. There was a possibility of a search he said and we had to make ourselves scarce. First, however, the cooking pots and pans had to be gathered, as well as the bicycle from the hayloft, placed together in a blanket and carried outside to a place in the forest where they could be buried while the search went on. With this we complied, leaving out a plausible number of pots and pans to deceive the enemy. Van Zieglers, for later I discovered what his name was, was evidently growing anxious. He had kept us in his house for two days now but still there was no sign or reaction from the Underground. We did as we were bidden and retired to the woods.

An hour passed, maybe two. I don't remember exactly what we did but after some time we were beckoned back again. The immediate threat of a search had passed but the pots, pans and bicycle remained buried. The weather was warmish and we sat outside for a change, between the woods and the cottage. We were smoking and talking of nothing in particular when an unexpected visitor suddenly appeared. We pricked up our ears and then stood to welcome her but she waved us down with a smile and came and joined us. 'Well,' she said, 'just the three of you is it?' She cast a look round the small circle, eyeing each one of us in turn. About twenty-two or three, with a light, belted mackintosh and scarf, she yet gave the impression of being much older, as though she had much on her mind. Her English, though fluent, was spoken with an American accent and she took her scarf off and played with it as she went over the points one by one. This was our first contact with the Underground.

'First,' she explained, 'you've got to understand that not

everyone is with the Underground. About ninety per cent of people just don't care; they want to keep out of trouble. Another five per cent are actively for the enemy. So that only leaves five per cent which is us.' She leaned forward to make sure that we were all listening. 'So don't speak to anyone unless you have to, you can't trust them. Have you got any escape maps?' To my great surprise, Pat Mahoney produced two or three. I was about to ask where he got them from but she pounced on them before I could speak. 'Ah,' she said, 'you know what to do with those, don't you?' The maps were printed on thin cloth and she took one and crumpled it up. 'You blow your nose on them and get them generally dirty so they can't be told from handkerchiefs. Like that you see?' She handed it back. We learnt, among other things, that the Allies were up to the Lower Rhine and the place we had come to was Uddel, about fifteen kilometres north-west of Apeldoorn. She had come to tell us that some clothes would shortly be delivered and in the meantime we were to stay put and await further instructions. I have a fleeting vision of a small, round face surrounded by dark hair, as she bid us goodbye and good luck. Then, she was gone.

That night we spent in the hayloft. The Van Zieglers family eyed us with a mixture of awe, fear and some apology as we were ushered up the stairs past the bedroom and into the loft, where there was more than enough hay to keep us warm. Gratefully we snuggled into the hay and fell asleep, full of hopes for the morning. For the first night that I could remember, there were no dreams.

In the morning, I was accused of waking the cow. I had snored so loudly, it seemed, that the cow had woken up, assuming that cows actually sleep and protested by lowing loudly in return. I looked round the faces one by one and all were agreed. 'But I can't have done,' I expostulated. 'You did,' replied Pat Mahoney. 'Yes you did,' said the Major and Van Zieglers nodded vehemently in agreement. 'Well, I am sorry if I did,' I said. 'Why didn't someone wake me?' But the three were laughing too much to answer.

CHAPTER 11

A Length of String

That afternoon, the clothes arrived and I had a brown suit. It fitted reasonably well and there was a shirt and tie to go with it. Our hospital clothes were taken from us for disposal elsewhere and we were now completely kitted out for our journey. The Major and Pat retained their boots and plimsolls and I now had a pair of black shoes, which had produced a blister within hours of their first wearing but beggars couldn't be choosers – it was no time to complain. We decided to give all our Red Cross food to the Van Zieglers family, after first removing the labels from the tins so that there would be no chance of them being identified later if another search were to take place. There was now nothing to do but wait. For three days, we had hung around the house and it seemed now that we were in for a fourth. It all depended on Dr Van Dawson, whom we never saw and who never came near us, and we were tempted to believe that he did not exist. That night we spent in the air raid shelter and, without doubt, it was the worst night I had ever spent.

Van Zieglers had dug a pit over which he had put railway sleepers, caulking the gaps with earth and covering the whole with turf. Into this cell of little ease we now descended to discover that, whichever way we positioned ourselves, we could not extend our legs or sit upright. Eventually, we sat in a row, with myself in the middle, and tried to get to sleep. Whether it was the cramped position we were compelled to take I cannot say, but I began to snore, whereupon Pat Mahoney promptly dug me in the ribs with an elbow to shut me up. No sooner had I nodded off again than I received another dig, this time from the Major. They kept it up at intervals through the night, sometimes striking in unison and growing more exasperated. In the end either I stopped snoring or they gave up, I'm not sure which, and we subsided into an uneasy slumber until dawn.

Some time before evening of the next day, when we were beginning to resign ourselves to yet another day's wait, two men appeared at the door and were shown inside. They had come, they said, to take us away on the first leg of our journey home. They waited until it was almost dark and then signed us to follow them. From the pocket of his mackintosh one of them now produced a length of string, one end of which he gave to the leader while he passed the rest of it to Pat, the Major and myself, taking the other end himself. We were at all times to keep a hand on this string, he said: one pull would mean stop, two pulls, take cover. We were then issued with firearms, in my case a heavy calibre .45 Colt Automatic, and off we set. We said goodbye to the Van Zeiglers family and I think they were glad to see us go; although they were friendly and helpful in every way, it must have been a terrible strain keeping us there night after night, not knowing for how long and expecting searches at any hour of the day or night. At least we had been able to give them our Red Cross rations; now we had nothing left to part with and we were wholly reliant on our rescuers.

At first the going was easy but as it grew darker so it grew harder and all we could do was to follow blindly, waiting for jerks on the string and now and again stumbling over unforeseen obstacles. We progressed in this way for an hour or two and then a definite jerk on the string told us to stop. There was a brief discussion in Dutch between the leader and the man behind me and then the leader set off in the darkness alone. We waited a while, not daring to speak to each other and unable to communicate with the second man, who spoke little English. After a period of about fifteen minutes the leader reappeared and with him were two others. The first spoke Dutch but the second none and next to no English either. Our team had increased from five to seven. The two joined the line ahead of me and we set off again.

By now we were passing through the woods again. A moon had risen, making the going easier at times and we pressed on at a seemingly increasing pace. At length there came a jerk on the string again and we lay low while the leader went up to reconnoitre. Then he came back again and we started off in line as before, soon to be ushered into a chalet.

We came into the building blinking at the light, which was low but enough to see by. All around us lay boxes, open and inviting inspection. In one were shoes, in another clothing and in yet another, Sten guns, pistols and ammunition. There were cigarettes and half bottles of Scotch and elsewhere, parcels of food and commodities like soap and matches. All these had been supplied by the RAF, dropped in the night and picked up by the Underground. We had moved into another world and were amazed and astonished, while our hosts relished our surprise, smiling at our perplexed faces and laughing at our exclamations. There was some talk of exchanging my shoes for a more serviceable pair but this was eventually dismissed as unnecessary. Then we turned our attention to the newcomer we had picked up on the way.

He was a Russian air gunner, shot down near Smolensk, and had made his way across most of Europe. One night, he said, when there were about two thousand in an open camp, the guards had got drunk and opened fire on them. He had escaped by playing possum until it was all over and had then got out through the wire fence. That had been in Poland. From Poland he had made his way slowly west, hoping to meet the Allies and give himself up. All this information had to be extracted painfully, in a mixture of Dutch and English, for none of us spoke any Russian. Exactly how he had managed to get across Germany was not clear but he had and finished up in Holland. There the Dutch had given him shelter and food, passing him from one house to another, until he ended up, alone for most of the time except when food was brought to him, in a hayloft. In the hayloft he had remained for eighteen months and had passed his time making trinkets, four of which he produced for display. We examined them in turn and, with smiles and nods of the head, congratulated him on his prowess. Beside his story, our own was next to nothing. He was an extraordinarily cheerful little chap and seemed very young for his age.

Our leader, meanwhile, had been sitting in the shadows, saying very little and taking in the scene. He was probably very tired by now and needed a rest before going onwards or back. He gave non-committal answers to our questions and, once again, we did not ask his name. He reminded me of a picture I had once seen of Rudyard Kipling, with a bushy moustache and glasses and a cap that never left his head. He was English, or apparently so. 'I expect to be back in England for leave at Christmas,' he said, seemingly unmoved and unimpressed by all that had gone on. I felt very much the junior boy. Now it was time to push on again, for the night, which gave us the cover of darkness, was slipping away and only a few hours remained until dawn.

CHAPTER 12

A Night Bicycle Ride

Four new escorts were provided for this next run. We set out this time on bicycles, each now armed with a Sten gun in case of attack. We sat on the carriers holding the Stens and facing backwards, while the escorts pedalled on slowly, keeping watch. We kept our ears alerted for the first sound of an engine, for any other transport on these roads at night would almost certainly be enemy. That part of Holland, on the way to Barneveld, was exceedingly flat and there were ditches at the side of the road into which we could plunge for cover if need be. It was an eerie sensation as we moved silently along the roads in darkness, wondering how far we had to go this time and knowing nothing of what our next destination might be. Slowly we passed on, mile after mile but meeting no opposition until we came to Barneveld. Here we split up. The Major went on down the road to stay with the schoolmaster, while Pat and I turned off to stay with the church organist. It was nearing dawn when we arrived at the house but the organist was awake and expecting us, as was another member of the Underground, a tall youth not much older than ourselves, in knee length black boots with an air of prompt efficiency.

We were shown upstairs to the top of the house and a door was thrown open. I have seldom received such a shock in my life. The room, though small, was indescribably neat and contained two beds with matching counterpanes. Laid out on each bed was a pair of pyjamas and, as though that was not enough, copies of books by Charles Dickens and Rudyard Kipling flanked by back numbers of *Punch* magazines lay on chairs beside the beds. We were immensely touched by this silent welcome and strove to make our feelings known to the organist and his assistant who eventually smiled and departed, leaving us on our own. It was quite light now and we undressed quickly and got into bed. From Uddel to Barneveld is about twenty kilometres, which we had covered, one way and another through the night. Sleep fell upon us almost instantly.

Some time later, we were woken up with a cup of warm milk and a small slice of bread and bacon, brought to us by the courier in the tall boots, who told us to come downstairs when we were ready, as a doctor was waiting to see us. We ate and dressed and went downstairs to a front room where a doctor was sitting. He examined Pat Mahoney's foot. After asking a few questions he seemed satisfied and turned his attention to mine. I remember bursting into 'giggles' at the time and being unable to control them. The doctor probed gently with his fingers and remained unmoved while I tried to explain, between fits of laughter, how the injury had come about. He must have thought me to be demented but carried on and eventually said that I should have medical treatment as soon as possible but there was nothing he could do at present. A small bone in the second toe of my right foot had become dislocated it turned out but it wasn't giving much pain and could wait to receive attention at a later date. I couldn't account for the laughter at the time. I suppose it was, in some way, a first opportunity to release tension that had built up during our escape. It soon passed off and I was back to normal again, or as near normal as one could be in the circumstances. We were, after all, still some twenty-odd kilometres behind enemy lines and anything could happen at any time. I put these thoughts out of my mind as soon as they occurred, choosing to 'bury my head in the sand' from the extremely dangerous backdrop to our activities.

After the doctor's visit we were sent upstairs again as the organist had some pupils coming. I read snatches of *Punch* but did not read Dickens or Kipling as I reflected that we might be moving on soon and I wouldn't have time to finish them. Conversation with Pat was sparse and desultory. I think we were both very tired. Finally we went to sleep again.

Morning came and with it more cups of milk and small slices of bread and bacon. I wondered for a moment whether this was a Dutch custom but reflected that it was probably due to a shortage of food. Lunch was pretty scant too, mostly vegetables. We ate every scrap that we were given but declined second helpings for we felt sure that we were stretching the organist's larder to its limits. After lunch we came downstairs again and soon afterwards received a caller in the shape of a policeman from Renkum.

He was a stout man with dark hair I remember and sat in an armchair placed a little forward of the organist's, looking from one to another of us with laughing but watchful eyes. His English was quite good and after a few questions and answers on both sides, he launched into a tale which, whether it was an exaggeration or not, most certainly held us spellbound. Two or three hundred *Gestapo*, he told us, had little by little assembled in a large house in or near Renkum. They had taken several days to arrive and were regrouping from France and Belgium before moving out to new stations. The Underground had got to know of this and had signalled information through to the Allies on the other side of the Lower Rhine. The Allies had reacted swiftly. During the night, a small force of bombers had flown over the river with three Dakotas bringing up the rear. These three aircraft contained paratroopers, who dropped in open country, while the aircraft continued on their way, following the bombers to another target and returning with them after the bombing to base. The ruse had evidently worked, for the paratroopers had not been detected. They gathered up their equipment and made for the house containing the *Gestapo*. This then they silently surrounded and waited until somewhere between two and three in the morning, when everyone but a few sentries would be asleep. Then they attacked. According to the policeman it was a massacre and few, if any, of the *Gestapo* survived. They were jumping out of windows, running down steps, fleeing up the street in pyjamas, only to be gunned down relentlessly in their attempts to escape. Satisfied at last that all that could be done had been done, the paratroopers withdrew across the Lower Rhine again. I think it must have been an American operation, for there were no British paratroopers left in Holland to carry out such an attack.

CHAPTER 13

Through the German Front Line

In the evening, when it was dark, we received a summons to set out on our way again, sitting on the carriers of bicycles once more but this time without Sten guns. It was only a short distance, we were told, and we were unlikely to encounter any enemy patrols. There was always the nagging doubt, though, and I don't think I could have carried on had not Pat Mahoney been there. He always appeared supremely confident and I wondered if he knew at that moment how near to breaking point I was. Well, if he could do it then so could I, was my spurring thought. There was no going back now, for better or for worse we were committed. The Underground escorts were always smiling and cheerful and seemed either to be unaware of the risks they were taking or to ignore them. What with their down to earth attitude and Pat's confidence, it seemed I was the only one who had any fears or misgivings. These I never communicated, knowing that to do so would be useless anyway. I was doomed to carry on now, come what may, and even laughed and joked a little at times, just to show that all was well. The Major, it transpired, was not coming with us but he sent messages wishing us good luck and a safe return. His wound had turned septic and he had been advised to rest his leg until it was better. We were never to see him alive again but did not know that at the time. We sent back our messages in return, for a speedy recovery and a safe journey home. How I wished I could have taken his place.

Eventually we arrived at an isolated farmhouse about six kilometres from Ede and I believe in the vicinity of Lunteren. Here

I felt a sense of relief again, for we were off the road and out of danger, for a time, at any rate. There were mugs of soup and chunks of bread to welcome us, which we ate gratefully, for some reason feeling inexplicably famished. We had arrived just at the end of an exchange of signals with the Allies over the Underground radio. We arrived just in time to see it being dismantled and put away. It consisted of a generator worked by pedalling a bicycle minus its rear wheel. The generator in turn worked the radio set, which sent or received messages with the Allies who were now up as far as the south bank of the Lower Rhine. When the whole thing was taken apart, there was nothing but a few innocent bits of bicycle and the radio, which itself was stowed away out of sight under some hay. Simple, ingenious and it worked. We returned our mugs and climbed up a ladder to sleep in the hayloft.

Years ago, it seemed, though in fact it was only five years, I had been to sleep in another hayloft. The day was warm and sunny and after lunch I had climbed up a ladder and decided to rest for a while. It was July or August 1939; war had not been declared then but schoolboys were encouraged to work for part or all of their holidays on a farm, to step up production for what now seemed an inevitable conflict. The work was not too hard and there were interesting diversions, such as driving tractors, thrashing corn or dipping sheep. Little by little I had succumbed to the beckoning fingers of sleep, not resisting much and had at length fallen into a rewarding slumber. Likewise I drifted into sleep now, notwithstanding the circumstances and forgetting for the moment the stresses of the day. There had been nothing more pressing then than the passing of a few exam papers, including a maths paper which, alas, I failed. This meant taking the other papers all over again and in order that there should be no misfire this time, I dropped history and took extra maths, which left long periods free for study in the library and always the Royal Air Force *Manual of Flying Training*. By and by, the shot-torn cities of Europe receded and I reminisced for a while about life in those days. Life had seemed halcyon in the summer holidays. I spent them for the most part on a farm near Merton, Oxfordshire, owned by a Mr and Mrs Deeley. Their daughter Kiki, I remembered, had been about three years old and we struck up a kind of relationship. We made paper boats for her once, floating them on top of the water butt and lifting her up in turn to see the fun. There was another boy, I remember, with glasses and together we lifted her up and put her down until, at last tiring of the game, we went off to our work and busied ourselves about the farm.

The next time I visited the farm I was a year older and had left school. One night, while on Home Guard duty in a slit trench up the road, a lone German bomber had come in search of Weston-on-the-Green. Either by chance driven from his formation or on orders from his command, he had droned over the sleeping countryside until he had reached his supposed target. An old man and I occupied the slit trench for part of the night and together we listened as the bomber drew closer. We could hear the desynchronised motors quite clearly now and although we could not see him, judged him to be pretty low, eight or nine thousand feet perhaps. Weston was reputed at the time to have a duplicate set of lights, so that, in the event of enemy attack by night, the genuine system could be switched off and the spurious pattern switched on. This they appeared to have done, for the German bomber circled slowly for a while, picking up his bearings. Finally he seemed satisfied that he had got the right markers and turned onto a new track, dropping bombs as he came. 'Thawacka, Thawacka, Thawacka,' the bombs fell in a straight line and seemed to be coming straight for us. 'Thawacka, Thawacka, Thawacka,' they went again, all the time coming nearer. No flak rose to meet him, no fighter intervened; the bombs were falling, as far as we could make out, on open countryside and heading for us. They then stopped and the bomber circled again for a while, as though searching afresh for his target. 'Do you think,' I asked, 'we could have a go at him?' My aged companion mused awhile. 'Well,' he said at last, 'I think we'd best not. After all, he might come down and have a go at us.' We had two .30 calibre American rifles with us and were scarcely best equipped to fire on a bomber, which we could not even see. Nevertheless, 'Just one shot,' I pleaded, 'we might get him, you never know.' My companion turned his eyes to the stars and surveyed the heavens slowly. 'No,' he said at last, 'I think us'd best let him be.' It was youth against old age, I thought. Oh well, the chance might come again. The bomber circled once more, dropped three more bombs a little further away and then droned off into the night. After we had been relieved and were walking back, I still couldn't let go of the idea of loosing off at him. 'We should have had a go at him,' I said, 'there was a chance that we'd have hit him.' 'Ah,' said the old man in reply and so the matter rested.

One day, with this same old man, I was privileged to drive the tractor up the village street, with a plough on the back, to a nearby field, which was ready for ploughing. It was not one of your modern ploughs with a hydraulic lift but one of the old fashioned ones, originally made to be pulled behind a horse but adapted by the blacksmith to function behind a tractor. As we neared the gate, the old man signalled me to stop. 'You'd best let I take her through the gate,' he advised, 'cause us don't want no trouble if anything goes wrong.' I could see his meaning and reluctantly obeyed. Descending from the tractor seat I ran forward to the gate, holding it wide open so that he could pass through. All went well until the tail wheel of the plough got caught in the gatepost. I am not quite certain what happened next but eventually the plough ended up in the ditch and so did one wheel of the tractor. Slowly the old man clambered out of the tractor seat and surveyed the scene of his error. He took off his cap and gently scratched his head. 'Cor,' he exclaimed at last, 'I reckon us have been and gone and buggered she.' It took two cart horses to pull the tractor and plough back onto level again; fortunately neither was damaged. The old man never spoke about who had done it, no one ever asked and I said nothing.

There was a girl on the farm then, an Irish girl with pale blue eyes and rippling hair, who used to do odd jobs about the place but mostly in the house. I know the girl's name but will not reveal it. One night I was perching pullets. It was getting dark and I had already perched two hutfuls, leaving one to go. Slowly I set about the task of putting up the perches one by one, at the same time sitting the pullets on them; you had to work slowly because if you didn't, the birds flew into a panic and jumped down from their perches again. It was laborious work, for no sooner had you got two or three perches in position than one bird would flop down to the floor again and have to replaced on the perch. When they were all perched for the night, I backed out of the door with a sigh of relief. It was then that I became aware of a girl standing there, arms crossed to keep out the slight chill that was coming on with the night and smiling at me. 'Did you get them all up then?' she asked. I stammered something to the effect that I had. I stammered because, for some time, I had begun to cherish a secret passion for this girl but didn't dare to express it and didn't know how to anyway. 'It's a lovely night,' she said. Exactly what took place next I cannot recall but I know we found ourselves in each other's arms. For a long while, it seemed like an eternity, we stood there and it was good to feel her body against mine and her lips parting into a smile before the next kiss. Then she quietly disentangled herself and put an arm in mine. 'I'll walk you back as far as the gate,' she said, 'and then I must go home.' As we sauntered back across the now darkened farmyard, all sorts of wild thoughts went racing through my head. She was the very first woman that I had held like that and I felt as though I were floating through the air. Gradually we reached the gate and kissed again. The next minute she was gone. I went to bed that night an insanely happy young man, full of dreams for the future and a warm, comfortable feeling where my heart should have been.

'Wake up, wake up, for God's sake!' It was Pat Mahoney shaking me by the shoulder. 'We're going to move off soon. They're waiting downstairs.' Gradually I opened my eyes and took in the scene – the heaps of hay, the roof, Pat, remonstratingly trying to wake me. Then I remembered where we were and there was anything but a warm, comfortable feeling in my heart! It was somewhere between half past seven and eight o'clock on a Sunday morning and we were still behind enemy lines. 'OK,' I said, 'half a minute.' I rubbed the sleep out of my eyes and sat up. It was a far cry from the girl at the gate. Fumblingly, I put on my shoes, stood up, brushed the hay off my suit and followed Pat down to the ground below. We were each given a mug of something hot to drink and another chunk of bread and while we ate we listened as they told us of plans for the next leg of the journey.

It seemed that this time we were to ride the bicycles with two guides out in front. We were never to come within fifty metres of them, so that if they were stopped there would be no connection between us, or, of course, *vice versa*. On the way they were to deliver a suitcase containing four pistols to an address some way up the road and while they were doing this we would have to wait for them to come out again. On their re-emerging, we should follow them once more to a point where they would leave us with final instructions for the next leg. We looked at our guides and I noticed how very young they were, fifteen perhaps, or sixteen. These were evidently the daytime guides, the night work was left to older men. I could not help reflecting how these and others, women included, were prepared to risk everything so that we should be able to go free. There would only be one end for them if they were caught, a firing squad, perhaps preceded by weeks of torture to worm out any secrets that they might possess. Were we worth it when all was said and done? Did we merit such unfettered service? They seemed to think so, at any rate. But they looked so young and smiled so unconcernedly that I couldn't help having qualms about their suitability for the exercise they were about to undertake. It was a humiliating thought but we had no choice but to follow. It was broad daylight now, on a Sunday morning, as we set off as planned with the two guides well out in front.

Slowly, all too slowly it felt, we made our way along almost deserted streets, heart in mouth, always with an eye open for trouble ahead, or around the next corner but contriving, I hoped, to look as though we did this kind of thing every day. Thoughts ran through my mind as to what we should do if we were stopped and questioned but, each time, I came up with a complete blank. We had no papers, only badly scratched identity discs in my case and nothing else. It was doubtful whether that would be enough to prove one's identity if the worst came to the worst. There was nothing we could do if we were halted now; we just had to trust to luck and hope against hope that it wouldn't happen. Round a bend we came, still in slow procession, and into a broader street, which kept us a greater distance from the houses on our left. As we were passing them, one by one, we came to a larger one with a German guard outside and were just breathing a sigh of relief at having passed it when suddenly there came a shout from behind. Pat and I stole sidelong glances at each other. 'I think we'd better keep going,' he muttered and I nodded in assent. Then there came a second shout. This time we, or at least I, waited for a bullet in the back but we kept on cycling, resisting the temptation to ride faster and all the time drawing further away up the road. There were no more shouts and no shots. Maybe he had been shouting at someone else, maybe not but at any rate we were past him now. We cycled on. At length the two ahead of us came to a halt and crossed the road, so we dismounted and I pretended to be fixing Pat's chain while he bent over and held a brief conversation. It was largely speculation about the shouting we had heard and whether I thought any more would come of it. I said I didn't think so; he was probably shouting at someone across the road but anyway, he was a long way behind us now and had most likely forgotten all about it by now. I honestly think I believed what I said; I know that I wanted to. Then we caught sight of another figure approaching up the same side of the road as we were. We returned to silence, becoming more engrossed by the chain again.

Casting covert glances at him as he drew nearer, I had seldom seen anyone in a greater state of disarray. He was a German soldier, with a pasty face and staring eyes and a cap that looked as if it had been put on as an afterthought. Without a shave for at least three days, with his expressionless features and half open mouth, he looked as though he had been on the jag for the better part of a week. His greatcoat buttons were all undone, as were his tunic buttons and as he slouched along with his hands in his pockets, he wore about him an air of hopelessness that beggared description. I also noted that he carried no weapons. When at last he came level with us, he vouchsafed a glance in our direction, so we gave him a muttered '*Morgen*' as he shambled past no more than six feet away and went on his way up the road and out of sight. 'Good God,' breathed Pat Mahoney. 'What the devil are they doing?' He was referring to our two guides who were still in the house. 'Probably out soon,' I muttered hopefully, fixing the chain for what seemed like the hundredth time. At last they reappeared and thankfully we resumed our ride.

This time there were no setbacks and we proceeded on our way, neither seeing nor hearing anyone. It was a strange sensation, cycling through the enemy-held territory on a Sunday morning, with little or no one in sight, an open road and nothing now in our way that I could see, for a bit, anyway. I began almost to enjoy a feeling of freedom, of wind ruffling my hair, of Pat Mahoney's company and the two guides out in front and was glad to have taken the decision that I had way back in Apeldoorn. What would come next, I wondered; another hayloft, a barn or a private house? It was good to be on the road again feeling free and with hopes of even greater freedom ahead. Now the guides were stopping again and this time they beckoned us forward until we came up with them and dismounted.

'This is as far as we go,' they explained, 'and you will have to do the next bit alone. Go straight on – do not turn left or right but follow the road. Eventually you will come to a hill. Go up the hill and turn off to the right at the top. Go into the woods a little way and wait for the next man to guide you.'

'How shall we know him?' we asked.

'He will be riding a bicycle,' they said, 'with a red cross on the front. He will tell you what to do next.'

We thanked them for all they had done for us and we shook hands all round.

'Good luck,' they said at last, 'you must be going now.'

Mounting our bicycles once more, we rode on again, a little uncertainly perhaps, but looking forward to meeting our next guide. By this time I had lit one of the last of my Craven 'A's, a gift from the party at the chalet, and we chatted quietly as we rode along, speculating about what our next move might be. Provided that we could make our next *rendezvous*, all should be well, I thought, for a time, anyway. I was beginning to relax at last and to enjoy a sense of well being. And then, out of the blue, came the first of our set backs. Pat was riding on my right at the time, when with growing horror we spotted some German soldiers lying by the roadside, some of them eating their haversack rations. 'For Christ's sake,' muttered Pat, 'ride on the other side of me. They may spot my army plimsolls.' We did a not too swift scissors movement and then held course. There was no going back now; we had to keep going forward. We kept on cycling at the same modest pace, our hearts in our mouths again and endeavouring to look as matter of fact as possible. A few Germans gave us a fleeting glance but most paid no attention at all. We cycled on until at last we came to an end of them, to where there was the beginning of an 'S' bend. 'Phew,' muttered Pat Mahoney and then 'Oh Christ!' came from me. We went through our scissors movement again, for this time they were lying up along the left side of the road. We cycled on, scarcely daring to look at the hundreds of eyes below us, some of them looking more interested than before, or was it my imagination? We cycled on, itching to go faster and get it over with but still restraining ourselves from taking a step that would undoubtedly have proved fatal. On we went, past the eyes, past the groups of NCOs and officers standing about chattering, until we came out into the clear again. My Craven 'A' had long since gone out but I had not dared throw down the stub until we were well clear of those curious eyes. Now at last, I threw it down as we made for the exit of the 'S' bend. There couldn't be any more now,

I thought, surely that's the lot. But I was wrong. This time, we didn't have to worry about the scissors movement, for they were lying on both sides of the road. They lounged there tiredly, as if waiting for someone to pass but evidently it wasn't us. One or two of them greeted us as we passed, so we replied '*Morgen*' in return, as taught, and continued on our way.

I was beginning to think that, if it were going to be like this all of the way to our next *rendezvous*, surely sooner or later we must be challenged. We couldn't keep on riding for ever through the German lines without being stopped but that is exactly what we did, for at last, we left the Germans behind us and breathed a sigh of relief again as we saw miles of open road stretching in front of us.

By and by we came to our hill and started up it, reaching the top a little out of breath and looking for a place to cut into the woods on our right. By mutual consent we chose one and dived off into what there was of the undergrowth but still keeping up our attempts to move as languidly and casually as possible, lest anyone should be watching from the road or elsewhere. The woods themselves were a bit thin here but there was enough cover to keep us hidden from the main road, while at the same time we could keep an eye open for our friend with the red cross on the front of his bicycle. Now and again a horse-drawn cart would pass, or a group of German soldiers would straggle by. Sometimes a motor vehicle would pass the other way, heading back the way that we had come. I was beginning to get restless again, wondering whether he had been stopped by troops or been delayed for some reason, when all of a sudden, we spotted him. As we reluctantly broke cover to greet him, he saw us too and hesitated momentarily. With the small red cross on the front of his bicycle now clearly in view, we knew that he had come at last.

This man was clearly more ill at ease than our companions of the road as he signed us to leave our bicycles where they were and follow him to the edge of the wood. This stopped about twenty-five yards short of the road, from where we had a good view of the traffic going up and down it. Waiting for a lull in the sporadic comings and goings did not take long and soon we were across the road and into the woods on the far side. We made our way over a short distance of no more than hundred yards and then broke cover. We could hardly believe our eyes. Faces turned to survey us as we stepped forward and we must have cut quaint figures, Pat in his dark suit, if I remember correctly, and me in brown. 'English?' inquired one of the faces. We nodded, 'And you?' 'Same here,' came the reply. We stared around us in bewilderment and disbelief. All about us were collected a galaxy of human beings, mostly in uniform, though here and there in civilian kit, like ourselves. There was a fox-like watchfulness about these people, eyes never looking in one direction for long before breaking off and looking in another, restless, wanting to be on the move all of the time; some cleaning weapons, others just relaxing but all on the alert. Some had managed to salvage a few firearms, while others had none. Some, like ourselves, had escaped, others had been on the run now for more than three weeks. A group of four wore handkerchiefs over their heads, knotted in each corner to prevent them blowing away. 'Hello,' I said jokingly, 'Playing pirates?' I was met with a somewhat briefly muttered response! It seemed that they had been living on the edge of a potato field for three weeks, not daring to move for fear of capture and living almost solely on potatoes, which they rooted out from the field after dark. Sometimes they cooked the potatoes but not often lest the smoke and steam give their position away. On the occasions when they had cooked, they had drunk the water that the potatoes were cooked in. This continuous diet had resulted in loss of hair, which they covered with the knotted handkerchiefs. While we were exchanging experiences, another figure joined the group, newly arrived from the road. He was smartly dressed in a suit, long overcoat and broad rimmed trilby hat. He had an unforgettable face with a hooked nose, which, all but met with his upturned chin when he smiled, looking rather like Mr Punch! He had been provided with fake identity papers, which stated that he was deaf and dumb. On his way along the road, he had been stopped by a German officer, with a suitcase and a bicycle. Quickly he had produced his identity card but had spent a frantic few minutes trying to understand what the officer wanted. At length it had turned out that the officer wanted help in getting the suitcase onto the bicycle and this they had achieved together, the officer finally making off down the road while our friend made his way to the *rendezvous*. He was an air gunner shot down somewhere over Holland and, like the rest of us, was attempting to make his way home again.

Nearby was the crew of an American Liberator who had baled out when their machine had failed, through flak damage, to make its way back to England. They kept very much to themselves and stayed together, not unsociably but because they did not feel entirely part of what was going on and watched and waited while others took decisions or made suggestions. Then there were about fifteen Dutchmen on the run from the *Gestapo*. These men also kept to themselves and we heard little and saw less of them as time went by. Lastly there were now two Russians with us, the one we had originally picked up from the hayloft and another, taller and bulkier, a huge figure in a belted leather jacket and a cloth cap. All together, we were about 110 to 120 souls, all with one aim in mind now – to re-cross the river and regain Allied lines. To have collected this number together at all was an achievement on its own; to have collected them, some in broad daylight and not a hundred yards from a main road, with German and other traffic passing up and down it, was something else; it was little short of a miracle. Some had cycled here, some had walked but some had come by an even more ingenious method. From time to time a horse-drawn wagon full of old people passed along the road. The passengers sat on long benches placed lengthways in the carts, with rugs over their knees, ostensibly to keep them warm. Under the benches and behind the legs was sufficient room for three or four passengers to lie in hiding and this is how some of our number had reached the wood. As though all this were not enough, in a far corner of the wood was positioned a German .88 gun, facing south across no-man's-land to the Allied lines beyond. From time to time this gun fired a salvo of three or four shells and attempts had been made during the night by British 25-pounders to sort it out; evidence of their activity was plentiful to see in the hanging and fallen branches and the scarred and tattered trees. Fortunately no one had been hit and in due course a message had been dispatched post-haste to the Allies, informing them of the presence of friendly forces in the area and asking them to desist. For the moment all was quiet, except when in the distance we could hear the sound of rumbling artillery, though which side was firing we could not tell.

CHAPTER 14

Operation *Pegasus*

There seemed little to do now but sit down and wait, which we did, uncertain of plans for the next move and awaiting instructions or information. Although it was 21 October it was quite warm and I think I nodded off for a while; anyway, the next thing that I remember was a call to lunch. At first I thought it must be a joke but it soon became plain that it was not. Crates of bottles appeared together with boxes of tinned food and now the whole venture seemed to take on the unrealistic air of a picnic. It seemed hardly credible that 120 people could sit down and calmly eat and drink with an enemy gun in the vicinity, while German traffic was passing up and down the road not a hundred yards away. The tins contained some kind of potted meat and the bottles assorted fruit juice, brought up the road by the same means as some of the escapees, under the seats of a cartload of elderly people. We ate and drank gratefully, at the same time wondering at the organisation that had been mounted on our behalf. After we had eaten, the tins and bottles were collected again but we were instructed to keep the corks, as these would be needed later on for blacking our faces.

Gradually the plan for the next move filtered through to us and sounded reasonable enough in theory. We were to move off at about eleven o'clock that night in single file and it was to be a case of 'follow my leader'; none of us knew precisely where we were going. We were to continue in this way until nearly midnight, which meant approaching the Lower Rhine somewhere between Wageningen and Renkum and the river crossing would be marked by two Bofors guns firing red tracer shells toward the German lines. At the crossing area American paratroops were to fan out into a protecting screen in the form of a semi-circle, through which we would pass down to the water's edge where boats would come and meet us. We were then to embark on these boats as quietly and as quickly as possible and make our way to the other side. It all sounded so simple and no mention was made of any enemy interference on the way. Just in case of any trouble, however, the party with weapons was to be put up at the front, otherwise, it seemed, no further precautions were or needed to be taken. Pat and I pondered over these plans but could find nothing wrong with them; we should just have to wait and see. Once again we settled down to bide time until eleven o'clock.

Once again the evil speculations entered my head and once again I did my best to put them out. They had a way of catching one unawares, stealing up on one and, suddenly, they were there. They seemed to be worse than usual this time but I had been coping with them for the better part of a fortnight or more and was beginning to get used to them. It was fatal to dwell on the future, for that might never come; it was equally fatal to dwell on the past, for that was over. What remained was the present and I struggled to keep my mind on that, with one ear cocked in the direction of the .88 in the corner and the other in the direction of the main road. There was absolutely no way out now, the thing had to be seen to a conclusion in one way or another; either we would be successful or else... Slowly the sun ran its course, the shadows lengthened, the evening came and then the night. We blacked our faces with the burnt corks, turned our watches face inwards, blacked the backs of our hands and then waited for our order to move. This was to be our last effort, our final bid for the Allied lines and freedom; after that, it would be England, home, and a rest from this strange existence that we were becoming used to; a return to sanity and things properly done. That, however, was dwelling on the future; with some difficulty, I dragged myself back to the present again. There couldn't be much longer to wait now, and then, all of a sudden, we were off. Stiffly, for it had grown somewhat chilly by now, we clambered to our feet and took our places in the long column that stretched ahead out of sight and into the darkness. Up at the front was the party with the weapons, then came the main body about eighty strong, followed by the American airmen, the fifteen Dutchmen on the run and the two Russians. We were, as near as could be judged, about two thirds of the way down the column.

Little by little we progressed through the night, stopping, listening, waiting and then moving on again. It was an agonising business, for we could only see dim shapes ahead and hear others coming up behind. We carried on like this until we came across our first obstacle in the shape of a small road, which we had to cross one at a time. There were big, grassy banks on either side, which helped a little but for 120 men to cross a road one by one at night, takes time and, when it came to my turn, it seemed as though an age had passed. However, we all got across safely and continued on our way, past sights we could not see and always trusting in our leaders. This time, there was no string to guide us. For what seemed like hours, we stopped and started, now crawling on our stomachs, then cautiously walking upright with eyes straining into the darkness ahead so as not to lose sight of those in front. Exactly how long we kept this up must have been a good deal less than it seemed but it was beginning to feel as though it was going on for ever. At last we came to a brief halt while a message was passed back down the line. It appeared that we were approaching a combined searchlight and machine-gun post, some two or three hundred yards ahead and situated on a small rise, which we could faintly discern in the gloom.

We were to turn our backs on this post as we made our way along the hedge at the bottom of the rise until we were out of danger, though exactly how we were to tell that did not figure in the message. By now, I had become outwardly calm but inwardly frantic; a kind of battle was going on between the inside and the outside but all went well until we came to a footbridge.

I could not see it properly to say exactly what it looked like but I remember it was small, not more than a yard wide, short, not more than eight or nine feet long, and it creaked! It creaked every time someone put a foot on it and it creaked when they got off on the far side. The creaks sounded louder in the silence of the night, particularly when we were bent on keeping as quiet as possible. To my ears, the creaks sounded practically like gunshots. Slowly, the column wound its way forward, each man crossing the bridge one at a time. 'Creak' went the bridge as each man crossed and 'creak' again as the figure disappeared into the darkness on the other side. It may seem a small matter now but at the time it was almost unendurable and I remember screwing myself up again and again to meet the next 'creak'. Something then happened, which I cannot account for to this day. I suddenly turned physically cold all over and, at the time, ceased to care about anything anymore. I didn't care whether the sun ever shone again, whether the Germans shot the lot of us, whether we crossed the Lower Rhine or perished in the attempt, or indeed, whether we ever got home again. We had come this far hadn't we? Well, it would be enough if it ended here, before or after the bridge. Did it matter whether we got any further? Definitely not. From then on, I pushed forward with almost complete indifference but feeling that I still owed something to the others, who I presumed fortunate enough not to feel as I did. When it came to my turn on the bridge, the searchlight was flickering a little, so I stood stock still and with ominous calm waited until it was clear that it was not going to shine my way; then I stepped off the bridge and the resultant 'creak' did not bother me one iota.

By and by we came to a hedge at the bottom of the rise to the searchlight and obediently turned our heads away from it as we filed stealthily past. Then we went downhill a little way, crossed another road, I think, and eventually came to some flat ground. By now it was ten minutes to midnight, so I assumed we were somewhere near the crossing area but there was no sign of Bofors fire. Oh well, I thought, just another let down. Probably no American paratroopers and no boats either but who cared? We had got this far hadn't we? It was then that the fun started. A German patrol, nosing about down by the river, had spotted some of our party and opened fire, fortunately hitting no one but causing temporary confusion. Our Bren gunner answered with a few bursts. Neither side could see each other but kept up the firing none the less. Bullets began to crackle overhead and then the Bofors came into action. Twin streams of scarlet shot across the sky, marking the crossing area and lighting up the scene. I stood briefly and admired them. Suddenly I felt a tremendous blow between the shoulder blades. 'Get down, you bloody fool! *Get down!*' It was Pat Mahoney and I think he probably saved my life at that moment. Gradually, the firing petered out, we got up and moved cautiously, ready at any moment to drop if the firing should start again. I didn't see any American paratroopers and so assumed that we had passed through their line. As we were approaching the bank of the river, which we could see quite clearly now, Pat Mahoney let out a sudden curse, his wounded foot having caught on something hidden in the grass at his feet. He turned crossly to see what it was and reached down for what turned out to be a beautifully polished, long barrelled, automatic Luger pistol. A sudden pang of envy seized me, to be followed by a feeling that, after all was said and done, he probably deserved it more than I. I still wished that I had found it just the same! Now was no time to be concerned with such things, however, for the last great obstacle, the Lower Rhine, was sweeping on its way before us, a formidable adversary indeed. There was now almost total silence, broken only by an occasional ripple or eddy, while we waited for the assault boats to appear, once again, straining our eyes into the darkness across the last strip of water that was dividing us from freedom.

We did not have long to wait before suddenly, almost under our noses, a boat came slowly into view. Its rowers had made the crossing in total silence and we now matched that silence as best we could as we clambered aboard. It was a collapsible assault boat, as far as one could tell in the darkness, which was about twelve to fifteen feet long, and I think about eight to ten of us piled into it, some of us taking paddles and pushing off as soon as we were all safely aboard. Once we were out into the main current, however, the boat suddenly swung sideways leaving us to paddle furiously on one side to maintain our course to the opposite bank. Progressing in this haphazard fashion, we finally reached the other side where some willing hands helped us ashore. As I stumbled out, a British voice in the darkness offered me a cigarette and then, as an afterthought, pressed an entire packet of ten into my hands. The next minute, he was gone. I looked around for Pat Mahoney but had temporarily lost him to the darkness. Gradually, I made out that a number of people were making their way up the bank and beyond, walking gingerly between two white tapes and then realised that they were walking through a minefield. I followed them and soon left the minefield behind. We came up to a road where transport was milling around with engines revving, ready for the 'off'. There was no time to waste, for we had to be out of the area as soon as possible in case the German patrol that we had bumped into had reported our positions. In such a case, we could expect some shelling. During the minor confusion an officer had his ankle broken but there were no other casualties and we soon clambered onto the trucks and were off on the road to Nijmegen. As the three-ton lorry bumped down the road, a sudden series of explosions in a field to our left made us jump and we were just considering what cover we could take when we realised it was our own guns firing back. Four 25-pounders were letting the enemy have it, hot and strong, and we hoped that they were finding their targets. We left them to it and took the road south-east.

Gradually the realisation began to dawn on me that we were free, that we had overcome the final obstacle, had put all the hiding, cycling and subterfuges behind us and could breathe, as it were, untainted air again. It took some time to percolate though and even then came through imperfectly, for I suppose we were too tired to take much notice of anything. My thoughts, too, were with the Underground, with the brave men and women who had risked their lives, not once but many times to save us. There was the elderly couple at the palace, Van Zieglers and his little family, the men on the string, the cycle rides, the church organist in

Barneveld and the guides who had finally led us to our last *rendezvous*. Without them we might have blundered around Holland for months, or fallen again into the hands of the enemy. Not yet for them the prospect of freedom, nor the welcome of a liberating army. They would go on, in spite of all odds, to the end, whatever it might be – liberation or the firing squad or sudden death. The RVV, for that is what the Underground wished to be known as, had served us for a while and would serve others to come in the future. In the meantime, we had thoughts of our own about our homecoming that they had given to us.

We pressed on through the night and some of us fell into conversation, even if we were a little too tired to make good sense. 'What did one think and do at the height of fear?' seemed the commonest question. 'I prayed,' I answered, 'just prayed.'

'That prayer business never did anybody a bit of good,' came a reply, 'it were a waste of time.'

'Well,' I answered, 'it seems to have got us this far.'

After that I think I fell asleep for a while. I was feeling dejected now that it was more or less all over, a curious dichotomy of feeling, with one half glad that the thing was done and the other wishing that it would perpetuate in some way. I woke up again as the transport was turning into the courtyard of the hospital in Nijmegen. It must have been some time in the earlier hours of the morning and I only have the vaguest recollection of arriving there, clambering out of the trucks again and being led up some stairs into a ward. Thence we were sent down with some soap and a towel to some showers in the basement and, on our return, to a bed with some pyjamas laid on it. I began to think of the pyjamas at the church organist's home in Barneveld and wondered how he was faring now. Our attention was next claimed by a plate of bacon and beans and, if I remember correctly, an egg to go with it as well. We ate slowly for we were very tired by now and drank coffee from pint-sized china mugs. We were not sure whether or not the coffee contained a soporific and didn't ever ask but we slept round the clock until the next morning. I awoke feeling a little dazed but managed to find my way to all of the right places to wash and shave with the razor that was provided and then return to my bedside.

Bits and pieces of uniform were soon being handed out to replace our civilian garments, which had been disposed of. Gradually I got together a pair of trousers, a shirt, socks, and boots but it was a long time before a battledress top could be found to approximate the right size. At last one turned up and a little later a nursing sister insisted upon sewing on one set of sergeant's stripes to the right sleeve. Thus attired, I began to feel a little bit like my old self again, except that I still lacked a headgear but none could be found to fit. Pat Mahoney acquired a black beret in addition to his battledress but wore no stripes and retained his plimsolls, as his foot was still giving pain.

One of the chief differences between this hospital and the one at Apeldoorn was that we were quite free to wander from ward to ward, up and down stairs and to seek out old comrades. In this way, we came across the little Russian again and Pat eventually agreed to part with half a crown in exchange for one of his brass charms. It was quite a struggle, for the Russian wanted some palpable evidence of his stay in Holland and his meeting with the British and he would only accept a half crown in return for the trinket; at last Pat accommodated him and he revealed the half crown like a gift from royalty. We tried to get news of the other Russian for he was nowhere to be found but to no avail. I thought that I had caught a glimpse of him at the river crossing, just before Pat had thumped me between the shoulder blades but I could not be sure. He was certainly not in the hospital, perhaps he had gone to another one. We bade farewell to our little friend but for some reason entertained misgivings about the other Russian. Was he a Russian or a Russian-speaking German planted to note the route so that preparations could be made to lay an ambush for when the next lot of escapees came that way? We decided that it was worth mentioning to the intelligence officer when our time came for interrogation.

After a while our turn was due and we were ushered into the presence of a young man who sat behind a table covered in maps, while we sat down opposite. I let Pat do most of the talking and, to my astonishment, he mentioned the name and address of the Van Zieglers family, which I had not known until that moment, as well as other addresses along the way. He then went on to outline, roughly, the last known position of the German tanks that we had encountered, which the officer noted, but he appeared to be more interested in whether we had seen anything like a launching pad for a 'V-1', the 'Buzz Bomb' that was plaguing Britain. Sadly we could not throw any light on that one but when Pat mentioned our Russian escapee, the officer hummed and hawed a bit, made a note and then passed on to other questions, which are less clear in my memory but few of which we were able to help with. The interview closed and the intelligence officer dismissed us with a cheery wave of the hand.

Some time during the afternoon we were invited to a concert given by the band of the Duke of Cornwall's Light Infantry, so we made our way to the hall at the far end of the building and sat on a windowsill to listen to them. The moving music of brass and tympani stole a sense of time away and led us into reverie. I was temporarily at a loss for words and thoughts and let my senses drift far away into the distant fields and pastures of my earlier homeland. I think it was the 'Lincolnshire Poacher' that did it. Then, with a jump, I came together and remembered where we were and how we got there and suddenly, unaccountably, felt a lump rising in my throat. It was quite persistent and I began to look for reasons to leave and go elsewhere but somehow stuck it out until 'God Save the King', clapped obediently, made my way out and eventually came to my bedside. Here, the feeling gradually subsided until I was once more at peace and *au fait* with the world of the present around me.

CHAPTER 15

Return to Britain

In the morning we clambered aboard trucks again and set off for Eindhoven, Pat in his battledress with a black beret and I in mine but hatless and with one set of stripes. As we drove down the road, we kept passing tanks upended in the deep ditches at the side of the road and I began to realise how stiff the fighting must have been to get through to the bridges at Eindhoven and Nijmegen, let alone to the bridge at Arnhem. They were German tanks and I assumed that the Royal Engineers had blasted them off the road to clear the way.

'It looks as though the RE have been busy here,' I remarked, 'blowing the tanks off the road.'

'Not the REs mate,' came the reply, 'RAF Typhoons.' The Typhoons were armed with 112-lb solid metal rockets. When the pilots dived, assumedly at a speed in excess of four hundred miles per hour and released these rockets, which also carried a propulsive charge, the impact as they struck their target must have been enormous and here was the evidence. Great, huge, massive things, brushed off the road like beetles and, once on their backs, like beetles doomed to lie on their backs and die. I stared down at them in wonder as we drove past.

Having turned a corner en route, we were driving slowly past a few farmyard buildings when suddenly, in a muddy yard, I saw a company of guardsmen at their drill. They were standing in open order and their spotless turnout made such a contrast with its background that, standing stock still and waiting for the next word of command, they looked for a moment like plastic effigies.

Behind and all around them were the relics and mess of war: mud, abandoned farm implements, a broken down wall, and a sagging roof. The heavy guns were rumbling menacingly in the distance but the guardsmen stood there as though turned to stone. Then, at a word of command that we did not hear, they moved from the 'slope' to the 'order arms' and stood stock still again. I could not help remembering then our own band that had crossed the river some nights ago, with blackened faces and hands, some unshaven and all but a few unkempt, who were now on their way home. I thought too of the countless hundreds who had died at Arnhem and Oosterbeek – gaunt, tired men, who had fought on against hopeless odds and then had fallen or had swum back across the river, endeavouring to escape the very jaws of death. 'Well your war is different,' I thought, as I eyed the guardsmen. 'Perhaps you have come to turn the chaos we have made into order. Perhaps you are the vanguard of a new regime, where all is order and reasonableness and happens by numbers, just as your drill does. Perhaps…' My heart was still with the battle-stained airborne troopers around the bridge at Arnhem, with the RVV and the last lap across the fields to the river. The truck continued on its way.

We stopped for a while in Eindhoven, not far from the giant Philips building, of which we could see little except the shell still standing and some parts of the roof still intact. From where we were it did not seem too badly damaged, although we could not tell the extent to which it had suffered inside. As we climbed down to stretch our legs, little children appeared from nearby houses and walked, smiling and happy amongst the troops and grown-ups came out and chatted where they could. It was a relaxed, timeless and happy scene, with no hustle or hurry about it, for the delirium of liberation had long since passed. For these people, the war was over now. For four or five years they had stuck it out, with lights failing, rations growing smaller, other food harder to come by, little or no heating throughout the winter and, above all, the continuous presence of the Germans. They had stuck it out and now the end had come and if all things were not immediately better, at least they were getting better and would do so from now on until they were back to normal again. They moved about amongst us and, here and there, a cup of tea or coffee was offered, and here and there a bar of chocolate or some chewing gum was given to a child. But soon the order to 'mount up' came again and we were once more on our way to the airfield.

At the airfield, we got off the trucks again and stood about, uncertain what to do next. There didn't seem to be much organisation but eventually we climbed on board a Dakota, along with some walking wounded and a stretcher case or two, took our seats, and waited. It was a British-operated aircraft, stripped of all but the barest essentials inside but to us it was one more step on the long journey home, for which we were consciously grateful. We looked through the portholes at the airfield outside but there were no longer any signs of the enemy occupation of some weeks ago, when apparently Prince Bernhard had attempted to land. At that time, the Allies were holding one end of the field while the Germans were retreating from the other and the Prince, blissfully unaware of the situation and in spite of all efforts to stop him, had approached to land. As his wheels touched the ground and he coursed on down the runway, he slowly became aware that he was being fired at and so immediately turned around and took off again in the opposite direction, downwind, clearing the Allied positions and making off for a more friendly airfield. It was indeed a flying visit, if in fact it took place. But we had no time to think of it now, for in a very few minutes, we were off the ground ourselves, wheels up and heading across Holland for the North Sea. We were flying again.

We looked through the portholes again at the ground below and it presented just the same picture as when we had passed over it more than a month ago. Nothing had changed and we flew over large fields surrounded by dykes and over flooded areas where the Germans had breached the dyke walls to hold up the Allied advance. Nothing could halt that advance now, it could only be delayed for a day or two, maybe a week, and then it would roll on again. Daily, more towns and villages fell into Allied hands as the relentless machine of war reversed the tide of battle and swept on, with ever growing momentum. Germany was doomed now and nothing could save her. Little by little, we left the land behind us as we crossed the coast and set out across the North Sea.

The sun was shining now and there was an almost cloudless sky. The old Dakota thundered doggedly on but for a moment I had a misgiving. What if a lone fighter should spot us, far out over the sea and 'down us' there, helpless, to become just one more statistic in an endless catalogue of disasters? For helpless we were; there was no escort, as there had been on the way in. Then the 'don't care' feeling returned again. We had got this far hadn't we? Then why ask for more? It was enough. We had proved that we could get out and back to our own lines. We had proved, whatever happened, that we had tried and succeeded. Well, that was that and nothing could change it, even if we were about to be shot down on the way home. Conversation was sparse as the engine noise was too great, so we contented ourselves with short dozes and intermittent glances at the sea in the sunlight. It stretched in all directions below now, without so much of a hint of land in sight, glassy in the sun's glow, with neither ship nor boat of any kind to break the seemingly endless pattern of the waves. From the height that we were, they looked only like ripples with an occasional, small roll of white to mar the illusion of a never-ending movement of eternity. By and by, we became aware of something thicker than mist on our port side and gradually, as we watched, it turned slowly into a solid and, as we drew nearer, into a coastline. It was England!

We now seemed to creep landwards, keeping all but parallel to the shore as we edged closer to the mainland. There were many speculations as to which part of the country we would touch down on – Norfolk, Suffolk, Cambridgeshire, Essex – but on we flew until, at last, we made a definite alteration in course and soon there were green fields below us. Slowly we began to lose height and I noticed how flat the landscape seemed and, was it my imagination, how much greener the fields looked than in Holland. At length we joined a circuit and could now see below us the airfield buildings, the control tower and hangars and, not far away, a village with a small church. My last impression was of a vast, flat expanse of green countryside and then, wheels and flaps down, we turned into our final approach. There was a moment of quiet as the engines ceased to throb and then we were down and rolling. Turning off the runway, the Dakota taxied over to the control tower, turned into wind and cut motors. We were home!

Pat and I climbed down stiffly and stood for a moment on the ground below. We looked around us, could not recognise a single soul in sight and hadn't the least idea where we were. We made our way over to the control tower and asked someone. 'RAF Barkston Heath,' came the reply. 'Where's that?' we asked. 'Lincolnshire,' came the reply. Lincolnshire! That was bad news; we were still a long way off base. 'Where's the sergeant's mess?' I asked and, on being told, we made straight for it without further ado. On arrival there, after what seemed like miles of trekking, we couldn't find anyone in to answer our call. Eventually, a corporal appeared. 'This mess is closed,' he said, 'what do you want anyway?' 'We have just got back from Arnhem,' I began. 'Where's that?' he asked, none too politely. Clearly, we were off to a bad start. Gradually, we got through to him who we were, where we had come from and what we wanted and he reluctantly agreed to do something about it. We were shown to an empty barrack room, provided with bedding and told to wait there until he came back. It didn't take us long to put our beds down and feet up and soon we were enjoying a snooze. It must have been somewhere between five and six when he came back, to inform us that there was a meal waiting. Pat and I eagerly followed him to the cookhouse. Somebody must have told him where Arnhem was, I reflected, for soon there appeared before us a plate of steak, piled high with chips, tomatoes and an egg. The steak must have been half the size of the plate. We struggled through this manfully, right down to the last chip, our stomachs not, by now, being used to such quantity but to only partially finish the offering would have seemed like an insult. We were then asked if we would like some more but asserted that we had now eaten more than adequately and asked tentatively whether there was a pub anywhere nearby. At this, Pat began to demur but I reminded him that we had been promising ourselves a pint most of the way back and he eventually agreed to come along for just one jar before turning in for the night. Following directions, we at length came to the pub and went inside. Pat ordered the first round, I forget now where we got our money from, and we drank our first mouthful of English beer for nigh on six weeks; not a long time by ordinary standards, perhaps, but at the time it seemed like an age. I think we managed a game of darts while the first pint was making its way down and then I ordered a second. Pat tried to stop me but, foolishly, I insisted. He was right. Try as we might, neither of us could finish the second pint. I struggled and struggled but could only get half way through the second glassful. Our stomachs had shrunk and were already straining with the large meal. We thanked and wished the landlord a good night, made our way back to the barracks and soon fell asleep.

I can remember little of the following morning. Pat Mahoney organised a Jeep and driver from somewhere to take us to RAF Broadwell and we set off on the long journey south. About half way we stopped in a town to stretch our legs, buy some cigarettes and have a snack. We were just returning from this expedition when we were stopped by the Military Police. We were improperly dressed, they said. I couldn't believe my ears. Improperly dressed after all that we had been through? I began to explain but Pat Mahoney got in first and delivered the most devastating attack I have ever heard. I wish I could remember the words that he used. By the time he had finished, the two MPs were standing to attention and all but saluting him. Pat then took his place by the Jeep driver and gave the order to drive on. There was silence for quite a while after that, nearly all the way to Broadwell in fact.

We drove in through the main gates of Broadwell some time in the evening and made our way to the sergeants' mess. My voice had been disappearing most of the way down and now it had gone altogether; all I could manage was a faint croak. Eventually I found a telephone and dialled my home number in Oxford to let someone know that I was back. After what seemed an indeterminable wait, there was a click at the other end of the line and I heard a voice say 'Here speaks Erna Plachte.' Erna Plachte was a refugee staying in the house and her English then was far from perfect. This fact, coupled with my lack of voice, resulted in further delay but at last I was handed over to my mother. Once again my voice let me down and my mother believed that it was a hoax. Try as I might, I could not convince her that it was indeed me on the telephone! I finally promised her that I would call on her the next day as it was too late to get any transport and left it at that. In the evening I went over to the mess again and there bumped into Ferelith, the daughter of the headmaster at Summer Fields School. She told me that her brother Hilary had been fighting with the Guards armoured column, trying to get through to Arnhem. The last time I had seen him, he had been dressed for a ball and was sporting an orchid. How times had changed, I reflected.

By the next morning I had kitted myself out again with wings, badges of rank and a red beret and cap badge and, feeling better for some breakfast, was now ready to 'set sail' for Oxford. I can't remember by what means I, at length, came back there but I recall turning at last into the house in Chalfont Road and ringing the doorbell. After a few moments, my mother opened the door. I was home at last.

After both of us had settled down, my mother told me that an old gypsy woman, a regular caller, had looked in while I was away and had seen that she was worried. 'It's a man, isn't it?' she had said. My mother replied that it was indeed and went on to explain that I had been posted missing at Arnhem, and since then she had heard nothing. The gypsy looked at her very hard for a few moments and then declared 'Don't worry, he'll be back. He'll always come back.' With that she had departed. My mother had hardly dared to trust her word but anything in the circumstances was worth holding on to, so she had lived in hope from day to day, waiting for news but as each day passed her hope had grown fainter. The next part of this narrative must sound incredible but, none the less, is true. Barely had my mother finished speaking when there came another ring at the doorbell. For some reason, I agreed to answer it and went to the door. There as large as life and showing no sign of excitement, was the gypsy woman. 'Ah,' she said, 'so you are back, I just thought I would look by and see that you're all right.' She refused all our entreaties to come in, saying that she had only called in to make sure that all was well, took her leave and was gone. Ours was the only house in the road that she visited that day, so how on earth did she know that I was coming? Even my mother had not known for sure. Following my telephone call, she had told no one, for she still believed the call to be some kind of hoax. Erna Plachte hadn't told anyone either. Strange, but we had to let it go at that.

My mother had one more surprise in store for me. 'I want you to tell me, if you can,' she said, 'what you were doing around midnight on October 21st. I've had a note in my diary.' She searched for and found the diary and opened it at the appropriate page. 'I woke up,' she explained, 'about five minutes to midnight, feeling that you were in terrible danger. So much so that I got up and lit a cigarette.' She went on to relate how, at first, the danger had seemed critical but the feeling gradually wore off and disappeared completely by about a quarter or twenty past. 'I made a note of it at the time,' she continues, 'just in case there was anything in it but I am probably just a nervy old woman. Afterwards, I went back to sleep because you seemed to be out of danger.' I was flabbergasted. 'October 21st?' I replied, 'I remember that date very well, because it was Trafalgar day.' I went on to tell of our last lap down to the Lower Rhine, the German patrol, the river crossing and the walk up through the minefield. 'But I wasn't thinking about you at that time,' I ended apologetically, 'I suppose if I were thinking of anything, it was probably about saving my own skin.' My mother put the diary down. 'Well,' she said, 'whatever you were thinking of, you certainly came through to me that night.'

CHAPTER 16

Summing Up

Certain people have asked me 'What went amiss at Arnhem? What was the cause of the failure? What do you think went wrong?' I must answer, first and foremost, as an ordinary soldier in the battle, that I saw the fight through my own eyes, was wholly concerned with my immediate fate and had no knowledge of the various events that were taking place within a stone's throw of our positions, let alone anywhere else. I did not know, for instance, that the radios had failed, or that General Urquhart was cut off for a time from the main force or that the main force was bogged down at Oosterbeek; I only came to know these facts much later. It is easy to be wise after an event and, much, much easier some forty years later. I have read *A Bridge Too Far* twice and seen the film twice. I have seen the film 'Theirs is the Glory', have read Brigadier Chatterton's book *Wings of Pegasus* and read General Hackett's book *I was a Stranger*. I have also read an account of the battle in *War Magazine* and General Frost's account in *A Drop too Many*. Extracting the facts from all of these sources, I am drawn to conclude that there was a muddle, a very serious muddle, which led finally to General Urquhart's remark to 'Boy' Browning: 'I went in with eleven thousand men and came out with two.' I think, also, that the muddle was due to the fact that the whole operation was planned in no more than a week or ten days at the most. It was hastily put together and there was a good deal of optimism afoot as well.

General Bernard Montgomery, as he was then, reviewed our troops at Bulford and afterwards drew us all in to listen to a speech laced, to say the least of it, with hyperbole. Of all the remarks he made, one has stayed in my mind ever since: 'I never attack unless I am two hundred per cent certain of victory.' To make sure that the message had gone home, he repeated it. Most of us present were not convinced by this remark and in the event we were proved right but at what cost! There were drops and landings, carried out over a succession of three days. By the time the second was due, the Germans, who were no fools, were almost ready for them. By the third day, shambles. All the newly arrived forces could do was to make for the now consolidated positions at Oosterbeek, where they remained until the end. Pat Mahoney for a long time clung to the belief that the whole disaster was due to 'careless talk' on the part of 'B' Squadron and, as I myself was in 'B' Squadron, I felt uneasy about this and avoided referring to the subject wherever possible. It was certainly not 'careless talk' on the part of 'B' Squadron that put the Polish Parachute Brigade down when and where it landed, or resulted in the container drops falling time and time again into enemy hands, or caused the radios to fail. The fact that the main force stayed bogged down at Oosterbeek and remained so for ten days, led to the final disaster, the loss of the bridge. The fighting there was horrific, as I now know, but I was saved that knowledge at the time by the fact that it was the first time I had been in action.

Of the Germans, I will say little but mostly to their credit. They fought like tigers and eventually, against a force gradually running out of ammunition and suffering casualties at an ever-increasing rate, they overcame. I am speaking now of the fighting at the bridge. The troops that we came up against were units of the SS, apart from a few *Volkssturm* reinforcements, who were dedicated fighters to the end. They, in turn, recognised that we were just as dedicated but fought well and hard for the possession of the bridge. I do not consider that any force could have held out longer than ours did, dogged by lack of supplies as we were but fighting on in spite of them. After all, we had done what we came to do and done it twice over; we had held on to that bridge for ninety-six, not forty-eight, hours and done it with a dwindling force of some three hundred men.

Henry Cole is gone now and so is Major Coke, shot while trying to escape a second time. Danny has gone too, blown up by a mortar bomb, which exploded at his feet. So have thousands of others; the roll call at the cemetery in Oosterbeek might well be a roll call of 'B' Squadron, to say nothing of the others who lie buried there. Of Bud Brailey, whom I mentioned earlier, I had cause to remember. During one of my many visits to various camps over the ensuing years, I chanced to run into some returned prisoners of war – among them was Bud. Fumbling in his kit-bag for a few moments, he at last withdrew an old airborne smock. It was a little the worse for wear and had the prisoner of war triangle painted on the back in indelible ink. 'Here you are at last,' he said smiling, 'I thought that you would like to have it back.'

As for Pat Mahoney, he was doing well the last time that I saw him, which was thirty-six years later at the Arnhem Memorial Service at the cemetery in Oosterbeek. 'Feel this,' he said, taking my hand and rubbing it along the lower part of his rib cage. I did so and felt a sizeable lump. 'Now you know what you landed on,' he said with a smile. As I felt it, I knew then that I had not landed, as I thought, on an iron rod, bent over to stop people walking on the corner of the lawn.

Written by Godfrey John Freeman, born on 4 June 1924 in Hook Norton, Oxfordshire. Freeman died on 9 January 1999 peacefully in the Churchill Hospital, Oxford, leaving his two sons Mark and Karl and their mother, his former wife, Sheila Freeman and his dearly loved sister Mary Sansbury who was awarded the MBE for her work raising funds for the Alzheimer's charity 'Brace'.